Post-Synodal
Apostolic Exhortation
of John Paul II

THE LAY MEMBERS

OF CHRIST'S

FAITHFUL PEOPLE

Christifideles Laici

On the Vocation and the Mission
of the Lay Faithful and in the World

BOOKS & MEDIA

BOSTON

Vatican Translation

IISBN 0-8198-4459-4

Printed and published in the U.S.A. by Pauline Books & Media, 50 Saint Pauls Avenue, Boston MA 02130-3491.

www.pauline.org

Pauline Books & Media is the publishing house of the Daughters of St. Paul, an international congregation of women religious serving the Church with the communications media.

6 7 8 9 10 11   05 04 03 02 01 00

Introduction

I

I Am the Vine
and You Are the Branches

*The Dignity of the Lay Faithful
in the Church as Mystery*

II
All Branches of a Single Vine

*The Participation of the Lay Faithful
in the Life of the Church as Communion*

III
I Have Appointed You
to Go Forth and Bear Fruit

*The Co-responsibility of the Lay Faithful
in the Church as Mission*

IV
Laborers
in the Lord's Vineyard

Good Stewards of God's Varied Grace

V

That You Bear Much Fruit

The Formation of the Lay Faithful

To Bishops
To Priests and Deacons
To Women and Men Religious
and to All the Lay Faithful

Introduction

1. The lay members of Christ's Faithful People *(Christifideles Laici)*, whose "Vocation and Mission in the Church and in the World Twenty Years after the Second Vatican Council" was the topic of the 1987 Synod of Bishops, are those who form that part of the People of God which might be likened to the laborers in the vineyard mentioned in Matthew's Gospel: "For the kingdom of heaven is like a householder who went out early in the morning to hire laborers for his vineyard. After agreeing with the laborers for a denarius a day, he sent them into his vineyard" (Mt 20:1-2).

The gospel parable sets before our eyes the Lord's vast vineyard and the multitude of persons, both women and men, who are called and sent forth by him to labor in it. The vineyard is the whole world (cf. Mt 13:38) which is to be transformed according to the plan of God in view of the final coming of the Kingdom of God.

You Too Go into My Vineyard

2. "And going out about the third hour he saw others standing idle in the marketplace; and he said to them, 'You too go into the vineyard'" (Mt 20:3-4).

From that distant day the call of the Lord Jesus "You too go into my vineyard" never fails to resound in the course of history: it is addressed to every person who comes into this world.

In our times, the Church after Vatican II in a renewed outpouring of the Spirit of Pentecost has come to a more lively awareness of her missionary nature and has listened again to the voice of her Lord who sends her forth into the world as "the universal sacrament of salvation."[1]

You go too. The call is a concern not only of pastors, clergy, and men and women religious. The call is addressed to everyone: lay people as well are personally called by the Lord from whom they receive a mission on behalf of the Church and the world. In preaching to the people, St. Gregory the Great recalls this fact and comments on the parable of the laborers in the vineyard: "Keep watch over your manner of life, dear people, and make sure that you are indeed the Lord's laborers. Each person should take into account what he does and consider if he is laboring in the vineyard of the Lord."[2]

The Council, in particular, with its rich doctrinal, spiritual and pastoral patrimony, has written as never before on the nature, dignity, spirituality, mission and responsibility of the lay faithful. And the *Council Fathers, re-echoing the call of Christ, have summoned all the lay faithful, both women and men, to labor in the vineyard:* "The Council, then, makes an earnest plea in the Lord's name that all lay people give a glad, generous, and prompt response to the impulse of the Holy Spirit and to the voice of Christ, who is giving them an especially urgent invitation at this moment. Young people should feel that this call is directed to them in particular, and they should respond to it eagerly and magnanimously. The Lord himself renews his invitation to all the lay faithful to come closer to him every day, and with the recognition that what is his is also their own (Phil 2:5), they ought to associate themselves with him in his saving mission. Once again he sends them into every town and place where he himself is to come (cf. Lk 10:1)."[3]

You too go into my vineyard. During the *Synod of Bishops,* held in Rome, October 1–30, 1987, these words were re-echoed in spirit once again. Following the path marked out by the Council and remaining open to the light of the experience of persons and communities from the whole Church, the Fathers, enriched by preceding synods, treated in a specific and extensive manner the topic of the vocation and mission of the lay faithful in the Church and in the world.

In that assembly of bishops there was not lacking a qualified representation of the lay faithful, both women and men, which rendered a valuable contribution to the Synod proceedings. This was publicly acknowledged in the concluding homily: "We give thanks that during the course of the Synod we have not only rejoiced in the participation of the lay faithful (both men and women auditors), but even more so in that the progress of the Synodal discussions has enabled us to listen to those whom we invited, representatives of the lay faithful from all parts of the world, from different countries, and to profit from their experience, their advice and the suggestions they have offered out of love for the common cause."[4]

In looking over the years following the Council the Synod Fathers have been able to verify how the Holy Spirit continues to renew the youth of the Church and how he has inspired new aspirations towards holiness and the participation of so many lay faithful. This is witnessed, among other ways, in the new manner of active collaboration among priests, religious and the lay faithful; the active participation in the Liturgy, in the proclamation of the Word of God and catechesis; the multiplicity of services and tasks entrusted to the lay faithful and fulfilled by them; the flourishing of groups, associations and spiritual movements as well as a lay commitment in the life of the Church; and in the fuller and meaningful participation of women in the development of society.

At the same time, the Synod has pointed out that the post-conciliar path of the lay faithful has not been without its difficulties and dangers. In particular, two temptations can be cited which they have not always known how to avoid: the temptation of being so strongly interested in Church services and tasks that some fail to become actively engaged in their responsibilities in the professional, social, cultural and political world; and the temptation of legitimizing the unwarranted separation of faith from life, that is, a separation of the Gospel's acceptance from the actual living of the Gospel in various situations in the world.

In the course of its work, the Synod made constant reference to the Second Vatican Council, whose teaching on the lay faithful, after twenty years, has taken on a surprisingly contemporary character and at times has carried prophetic significance. Such teaching has the capacity to enlighten and guide the responses which today must be given to new situations. In reality, the challenge embraced by the Synod Fathers has been that of indicating the concrete ways through which this rich "theory" on the lay state expressed by the Council can be translated into authentic Church "practice." Some situations have made themselves felt because of a certain "novelty" that they have, and in this sense they can be called post-conciliar—at least chronologically; to these the Synod Fathers have rightly given a particular attention in the course of their discussion and reflection. Among the situations to be recalled are those regarding the ministries and Church services entrusted at present and in the future to the lay faithful; the growth and spread of new "movements" alongside other group forms of lay involvement; and the place and role of women both in the Church and in society.

At the conclusion of their work, which proceeded with great commitment, competence and generosity, the Synod Fathers made known to me their desires and requested that at an opportune time, a conclusive papal document on the topic of the lay faithful be offered to the Universal Church.[5]

This Post-Synodal Apostolic Exhortation intends to take into account all the richness of the Synod work, from the *Lineamenta* to the *Instrumentum Laboris;* from the introductory report, the presentations of individual bishops and lay persons to the summary reports after discussion in the Synod hall; from the discussions and reports of the "small groups" to the final "Propositions" and the concluding "Message." For this reason the present document is not something in contradistinction to the Synod, but is meant to be a faithful and coherent expression of it—a fruit of collegiality. As such, the Council of the General Secretariat of the Synod of Bishops and the Secretariat itself have contributed to its final form.

This Exhortation intends to stir and promote a deeper awareness among all the faithful of the gift and responsibility they share, both as a group and as individuals, in the communion and mission of the Church.

The Pressing Needs of the World Today: "Why Do You Stand Here Idle All Day?"

3. The basic meaning of this Synod and the most precious fruit desired as a result of it, is the *lay faithful's hearkening to the call of Christ the Lord to work in his vineyard,* to take an active, conscientious and responsible part in the mission of the Church *in this great moment in history,* made especially dramatic by occurring on the threshold of the Third Millennium.

A new state of affairs today both in the Church and in social, economic, political and cultural life, calls with a particular urgency for the action of the lay faithful. If lack of commitment is always unacceptable, the present time renders it even more so. *It is not permissible for anyone to remain idle.*

We continue in our reading of the gospel parable: "And about the eleventh hour he went out and found others standing; and he said to them, 'Why do you stand here idle all day?' They said to him, 'Because no one has hired us.' He said to them, 'You too go into the vineyard'" (Mt 20:6-7).

Since the work that awaits everyone in the vineyard of the Lord is so great, there is no place for idleness. With even greater urgency the "householder" repeats his invitation: "you too go into my vineyard."

The voice of the Lord clearly resounds in the depths of each of Christ's followers who, through faith and the sacraments of Christian initiation is made like to Jesus Christ, is incorporated as a living member in the Church and has an active part in her mission of salvation. The voice of the Lord also comes to be heard through the historic events of the Church and humanity as the Council reminds us: "The People of God believes that it is led by the Spirit of the Lord who fills the whole world. Moved by this faith it tries to discern authentic signs of God's presence and purpose in the events, the needs, and the longings which it shares with other people of our time. For faith throws a new light on all things and makes known the full ideal to which God has called each individual, and

15

thus guides the mind towards solutions which are fully human."[6]

It is necessary, then, to keep a watchful eye on this our world, with its problems and values, its unrest and hopes, its defeats and triumphs: a world whose economic, social, political and cultural affairs pose problems and grave difficulties in light of the description provided by the Council in the Pastoral Constitution, *Gaudium et Spes*.[7] *This* then, is the vineyard; *this* is the field in which the faithful are called to fulfill their mission. Jesus wants them, as he wants all his disciples, to be the "salt of the earth" and the "light of the world" (cf. Mt 5:13-14). But what is the *actual state of affairs* of the "earth" and the "world," for which Christians ought to be "salt" and "light"?

The variety of situations and problems that exist in our world is indeed great and rapidly changing. For this reason it is all the more necessary to guard against generalizations and unwarranted simplifications. It is possible, however, to highlight *some trends that are emerging in present-day society.* The Gospel records that the weeds and the good grain grew together in the farmer's field. The same is true in history where in everyday life there often exist contradictions in the exercise of human freedom, where there is found side by side and at times closely intertwined, evil and good, injustice and justice, anguish and hope.

Secularism and the Need for Religion

4. How can one not notice the ever-growing existence of *religious indifference* and *atheism* in its more varied forms particularly in its perhaps

most widespread form of *secularism?* Adversely affected by the impressive triumphs of continuing scientific and technological development and above all, fascinated by a very old and yet new temptation, namely, that of wishing to become like God (cf. Gen 3:5) through the use of a liberty without bounds, individuals cut the religious roots that are in their hearts; they forget God or simply retain him without meaning in their lives, or outrightly reject him and begin to adore various "idols" of the contemporary world.

The present-day phenomenon of secularism is truly serious not simply as regards the individual, but in some ways as regards whole communities, as the Council has already indicated: "Growing numbers of people are abandoning religion in practice."[8] At other times I myself have recalled the phenomenon of de-Christianization which strikes long-standing Christian people and which continually calls for a re-evangelization.

Human longing and the need for religion, however, are not able to be totally extinguished. When persons in conscience have the courage to face the more serious questions of human existence—particularly questions related to the purpose of life, to suffering and to dying—they are unable to avoid making their own the words of truth uttered by St. Augustine: "You have made us for yourself, O Lord, and our hearts are restless until they rest in you."[9] In the same manner the present-day world bears witness to this as well, in ever-increasing and impressive ways, through an openness to a spiritual and transcendent outlook towards life; the renewed interest in religious research; the return to a sense of the sacred and to prayer; and the demand for freedom to call upon the name of the Lord.

The Human Person:
A Dignity Violated and Exalted

5. We furthermore call to mind the *violations* to which the human person is subjected.

When the individual is not recognized and loved in the person's dignity as the living image of God (cf. Gen 1:26), the human being is exposed to more humiliating and degrading forms of "manipulation," that most assuredly reduce the individual to a slavery to those who are stronger. "Those who are stronger" can take a variety of names: an ideology, economic power, political and inhumane systems, scientific technocracy or the intrusiveness of the mass-media. Once again we find ourselves before many persons—our sisters and brothers—whose fundamental rights are being violated, owing to their exceedingly great capacity for endurance and to the clear injustice of certain civil laws: the right to life and to integrity; the right to a house and to work; the right to a family and responsible parenthood; the right to participation in public and political life; the right to freedom of conscience and the practice of religion.

Who is able to count the number of babies unborn because they have been killed in their mothers' wombs, children abandoned and abused by their own parents, children who grow without affection and education? In some countries entire populations are deprived of housing and work, lacking the means absolutely essential for leading a life worthy of a human being, and are deprived even of those things necessary for their sustenance. There are great areas of poverty and of misery, both physical and moral, existing at this moment on the periphery of great cities. Entire groups of human beings have been seriously afflicted.

But the *sacredness of the human person* cannot be obliterated no matter how often it is devalued and violated because it has its unshakable foundation in God as Creator and Father. The sacredness of the person always keeps returning again and again.

The sense of the dignity of the human person must be pondered and reaffirmed in stronger terms. A beneficial trend is advancing and permeating all peoples of the earth, making them ever more aware of the dignity of the individual: the person is not at all a "thing" or an "object" to be used, but primarily a responsible "subject," one endowed with conscience and freedom; called to live responsibly in society and history; and oriented towards spiritual and religious values.

It has been said that ours is the time of "humanism": paradoxically, some of its atheistic and secularistic forms arrive at a point where the human person is diminished and annihilated; other forms of humanism, instead, exalt the individual in such a manner that these forms become a veritable and real idolatry. There are still other forms, however, in line with the truth, which rightly acknowledge the greatness and misery of individuals and manifest, sustain and foster the total dignity of the human person.

The sign and fruit of this trend towards humanism is the growing need for *participation* which is undoubtedly one of the distinctive features of present-day humanity, a true "sign of the times" that is developing in various fields and in different ways; above all the growing need for participation regarding women and young people, not only in areas of family and academic life, but also in cultural, economic, social and political areas. To be leading characters in this development—in some ways to be creators of a new, more humane culture—is a requirement both for the individual and for peoples as a whole.[10]

Conflict and Peace

6. Finally, we are unable to overlook another phenomenon that is quite evident in present-day humanity: perhaps as never before in history, humanity is daily buffetted by *conflict*. This is a phenomenon which has many forms, displayed in a legitimate plurality of mentalities and initiatives, but manifested in the fatal opposition of persons, groups, categories, nations and blocks of nations. This opposition takes the form of violence, of terrorism, and of war. Once again, but with proportions enormously widespread, diverse sectors of humanity today, wishing to show their "omnipotence," renew the futile experience of constructing the "Tower of Babel" (cf. Gen 11:1-9) which spreads confusion, struggle, disintegration and oppression. The human family is thus in itself dramatically convulsed and wounded.

On the other hand, totally unsuppressible is that human longing experienced by individuals and whole peoples for the inestimable good of *peace* in justice. The gospel beatitude: "Blessed are the peacemakers" (Mt 5:9) finds in the people of our time a new and significant resonance: entire populations today live, suffer and labor to bring about peace and justice. The *participation* by so many persons and groups in the life of society is increasingly pursued today as the way to make a desired peace become a reality. On this road we meet many lay faithful generously committed to the social and political field, working in a variety of institutional forms and those of a voluntary nature in service to the least.

Jesus Christ, the Hope of Humanity

7. This then, is the vast field of labor that stands before the laborers sent forth by the "householder" to work in his vineyard.

In this field the Church is present and working, everyone of us—pastors, priests, deacons, religious and lay faithful. The adverse situations here mentioned deeply affect the Church: they in part condition the Church, but they do not crush her, nor even less overcome her because the Holy Spirit, who gives her life, sustains her in her mission.

Despite every difficulty, delay and contradiction caused by the limits of human nature, by sin and by the Evil One, the Church knows that all the forces that humanity employs for communion and participation find a full response in the intervention of Jesus Christ, the Redeemer of man and of the world.

The Church knows that she is sent forth by him as "sign and instrument of intimate union with God and of the unity of all the human race."[11]

Despite all this humanity is able to hope. Indeed it must hope: the living and personal Gospel, *Jesus Christ himself, is the "good news" and the bearer of joy* that the Church announces each day, and to whom the Church bears testimony before all people.

The lay faithful have an essential and irreplaceable role in this announcement and in this testimony: through them the Church of Christ is made present in the various sectors of the world as a sign and source of hope and of love.

I

I Am the Vine
and You Are the Branches

*The Dignity of the Lay Faithful
in the Church as Mystery*

The Mystery of the Vine

8. The Sacred Scriptures use the image of the vine in various ways. In a particular case, the vine serves to express the *Mystery of the People of God.* From this perspective which emphasizes the Church's internal nature, the lay faithful are seen not simply as laborers who work in the vineyard, but as themselves being a part of the vineyard. Jesus says, "I am the vine, you are the branches" (Jn 15:5).

The prophets in the Old Testament used the image of the vine to describe the chosen people. Israel is God's vine, the Lord's own work, the joy of his heart: "I have planted you a choice vine" (Jer 2:21); "Your mother was like a vine in a vineyard transplanted by the water, fruitful and full of branches by reason of abundant water" (Ez 19:10); "My beloved had a vineyard on a very fertile hill. He dug it and cleared it of stones and planted it with choice vines..." (Is 5:1-2).

Jesus himself once again takes up the symbol of the vine and uses it to illustrate various aspects of the Kingdom of God: "A man planted a vineyard, and set a hedge around it, and dug a pit for the winepress, and built a tower and let it out to tenants and went into another country" (Mk 12:1; cf. Mt 21:28ff.).

John the Evangelist invites us to go further and leads us to discover *the mystery of the vine:* it is the figure and symbol not only of the People of God, but of *Jesus himself.* He is the vine and we, his disciples, are the branches. He is the "true vine," to which the branches are engrafted to have life (cf. Jn 15:1ff.).

The Second Vatican Council, making reference to the various biblical images that help to reveal the mystery of the Church, proposes again the image of the vine and the branches: "Christ is the true vine who gives life and fruitfulness to the branches, that is, to us. Through the Church we abide in Christ, without whom we can do nothing (Jn 15:1-5)." [12] The Church herself, then, is the vine in the Gospel. She is *mystery* because the very life and love of the Father, Son and Holy Spirit are the gift gratuitously offered to all those who are born of water and the Holy Spirit (cf. Jn 3:5), and called to relive the very *communion* of God and to manifest it and communicate it in history (mission): "In that day," Jesus says, "you will know that I am in my Father and you in me, and I in you" (Jn 14:20).

Only *from inside the Church's mystery of communion is the "identity" of the lay faithful made known* and their fundamental dignity revealed. Only within the context of this dignity can their vocation and mission in the Church and in the world be defined.

Who Are the Lay Faithful?

9. The Synod Fathers have rightly pointed to the need for a definition of the lay faithful's vocation and mission in *positive terms* through an in-depth study of the teachings of the Second Vatican Council in light of both recent documentation from the Magisterium and the lived experience of the Church, guided as she is by the Holy Spirit.[13]

In giving a response to the question "Who are the lay faithful?" the Council went beyond previous interpretations which were predominantly negative. Instead it opened itself to a decidedly positive vision and displayed a basic intention of asserting *the full belonging of the lay faithful to the Church and to its mystery. At the same time it insisted on the unique character of their vocation* which is, in a special way, to "seek the Kingdom of God by engaging in temporal affairs and ordering them according to the plan of God."[14] "The term 'lay faithful'"—we read in the Constitution on the Church, *Lumen Gentium*—"is here understood to mean all the faithful except those in Holy Orders and those who belong to a religious state sanctioned by the Church. Through Baptism the lay faithful are made one body with Christ and are established among the People of God. They are in their own way made sharers in the priestly, prophetic and kingly office of Christ. They carry out their own part in the mission of the whole Chris-

25

tian people with respect to the Church and the world." [15]

Pius XII once stated: "The Faithful, more precisely the lay faithful, find themselves on the front lines of the Church's life; for them the Church is the animating principle for human society. Therefore, they in particular, ought to have an ever-clearer consciousness *not only of belonging to the Church, but of being the Church,* that is to say, the community of the faithful on earth under the leadership of the Pope, the head of all, and of the Bishops in communion with him. These *are the Church....*" [16]

According to the biblical image of the vineyard, the lay faithful, together with all the other members of the Church, are branches engrafted to Christ the true vine, and from him derive their life and fruitfulness.

Incorporation into Christ through faith and Baptism is the source of being a Christian in the mystery of the Church. This mystery constitutes the Christian's most basic "features" and serves as the basis for all the vocations and dynamism of the Christian life of the lay faithful (cf. Jn 3:5). In Christ who died and rose from the dead, the baptized become a "new creation" (Gal 6:15; 2 Cor 5:17), washed clean from sin and brought to life through grace.

Therefore, only through accepting the richness in mystery that God gives to the Christian in Baptism is it possible to come to a basic description of the lay faithful.

Baptism and the "Newness" of Christian Life

10. It is no exaggeration to say that the entire existence of the lay faithful has as its purpose to lead a person to a knowledge of the radical newness of the Christian life that comes from Baptism, the sacrament of faith, so that this knowledge can help that person live the responsibilities which arise from that vocation received from God. In arriving at a basic description of the lay faithful we now more explicitly and directly consider among others the following three fundamental aspects: *Baptism regenerates us in the life of the Son of God; unites us to Christ and to his Body, the Church; anoints us in the Holy Spirit, making us spiritual temples.*

Children in the Son

11. We here recall Jesus' words to Nicodemus: "Truly, truly, I say to you, unless one is born of water and the Spirit, he cannot enter the kingdom of God" (Jn 3:5). Baptism, then, is a rebirth, a regeneration.

In considering this aspect of the gift which comes from Baptism, the Apostle Peter breaks out into song: "Blessed be the God and Father of our Lord Jesus Christ! By his great mercy we have been born anew to a living hope through the resurrection of Jesus Christ from the dead and to an inheritance which is imperishable, undefiled and unfading" (1 Pt 1:3-4). And he calls Christians those who have been "born anew, not of perishable seed but of imperishable, through the living and abiding word of God" (1 Pt 1:23).

With Baptism we become *children of God in his only-begotten Son, Jesus Christ.* Rising from the waters of the baptismal font, every Christian hears again the voice that was once heard on the banks of the Jordan River: "You are my beloved Son; with you I am well pleased" (Lk 3:22). From this comes the understanding that one has been brought into association with the beloved Son, becoming a child of adoption (cf. Gal 4:4-7) and a brother or sister of Christ. In this way the eternal plan of the Father for each person is realized in history: "For those whom he foreknew he also predestined to be conformed to the image of his Son, in order that he might be the first-born among many brethren" (Rom 8:29).

It is the *Holy Spirit* who constitutes the baptized as Children of God and members of Christ's Body. St. Paul reminds the Christians of Corinth of this fact: "For by one Spirit we are all baptized into one body" (1 Cor 12:13), so that the Apostle can say to the lay faithful: "Now you are the body of Christ and individually members of it" (1 Cor 12:27); "and because you are sons, God has sent the Spirit of his Son into our hearts" (Gal 4:6; cf. Rom 8:15-16).

We Are One Body in Christ

12. Regenerated as "Children in the Son," the baptized are inseparably joined together as *"members of Christ and members of the body of the Church,"* as the Council of Florence teaches.[17]

Baptism symbolizes and brings about a mystical but real incorporation into the crucified and glorious body of Christ. Through the sacrament

Jesus unites the baptized to his death so as to unite the recipient to his resurrection (cf. Rom 6:3-5). The "old man" is stripped away for a reclothing with "the new man," that is, with Jesus himself: "For as many of you as were baptized into Christ have put on Christ" (Gal 3:27; cf. Eph 4:22-24; Col 3:9-10). The result is that "we, though many, are one body in Christ" (Rom 12:5).

In the words of St. Paul we find again the faithful echo of the teaching of Jesus himself which reveals *the mystical unity of Christ with his disciples and the disciples with each other,* presenting it as an image and extension of that mystical *communion* that binds the Father to the Son and the Son to the Father in the bond of love, the Holy Spirit (cf. Jn 17:21). Jesus refers to this same unity in the image of the vine and the branches: "I am the vine, you the branches" (Jn 15:5), an image that sheds light not only on the deep intimacy of the disciples with Jesus but on the necessity of a vital communion of the disciples with each other: all are branches of a single vine.

Holy and Living Temples of the Spirit

13. In another comparison, using the image of a building, the Apostle Peter defines the baptized as "living stones" founded on Christ, the "corner stone," and destined to "be raised up into a spiritual building" (1 Pt 2:5ff.). The image introduces us to another aspect of the newness of Christian life coming from Baptism and described by the Second Vatican Council: "By regeneration and the anointing of the Holy Spirit, the baptized are consecrated into a spiritual house."[18]

The Holy Spirit "anoints" the baptized, sealing each with an indelible character (cf. 2 Cor 1:21-22), and constituting each as a spiritual temple, that is, he fills this temple with the holy presence of God as a result of each person's being united and likened to Jesus Christ.

With this spiritual "unction," Christians can repeat in an individual way the words of Jesus: "The Spirit of the Lord is upon me, because he has anointed me to preach the good news to the poor. He has sent me to proclaim release to captives and recovery of sight to the blind, to set at liberty those who are oppressed, to proclaim the acceptable year of the Lord" (Lk 4:18-19; cf. Is 61:1-2). Thus with the outpouring of the Holy Spirit in Baptism and Confirmation, the baptized share in the same mission of Jesus as the Christ, the Savior-Messiah.

Sharers in the Priestly, Prophetic and Kingly Mission of Jesus Christ

14. Referring to the baptized as "newborn babes," the Apostle Peter writes: "Come to him, to that living stone, rejected by men but in God's sight chosen and precious; and like living stones be yourselves built into a spiritual house, to be a holy priesthood to offer spiritual sacrifices acceptable to God through Jesus Christ...you are a chosen race, a royal priesthood, a holy nation, God's own people, that you may declare the wonderful deeds of him who called you out of darkness into his marvelous light" (1 Pt 2:4-5, 9).

A new aspect to the grace and dignity coming from Baptism is here introduced: the lay faithful participate, for their part, in the threefold mission of Christ as Priest, Prophet and King. This aspect has never been forgotten in the living tradition of the Church, as exemplified in the explanation which St. Augustine offers for Psalm 26: "David was anointed king. In those days only a king and a priest were anointed. These two persons prefigured the one and only priest and king who was to come, Christ (the name "Christ" means "anointed"). Not only has our head been anointed but we, his body, have also been anointed...therefore *anointing* comes to all Christians, even though in Old Testament times it belonged only to two persons. Clearly we are the Body of Christ because we are all "anointed" and in him are "christs," that is, "anointed ones," as well as Christ himself, "The Anointed One." In a certain way, then, it thus happens that with head and body the whole Christ is formed."[19]

In the wake of the Second Vatican Council,[20] at the beginning of my pastoral ministry, my aim was to emphasize forcefully the priestly, prophetic and kingly dignity of the entire People of God in the following words: "He who was born of the Virgin Mary, the carpenter's Son—as he was thought to be—Son of the living God (confessed by Peter), has come to make us 'a kingdom of priests.' The Second Vatican Council has reminded us of the mystery of this power and of the fact that the mission of Christ—Priest, Prophet-Teacher, King—continues in the Church. Everyone, the whole People of God, shares in this threefold mission."[21]

With this Exhortation the lay faithful are invited to take up again and reread, meditate on and assimilate with renewed understanding and love, the rich and fruitful teaching of the Council which speaks of their participation in the threefold mission of Christ.[22] Here in summary form are the essential elements of this teaching.

The lay faithful are sharers in the *priestly mission* for which Jesus offered himself on the cross and continues to be offered in the celebration of the Eucharist for the glory of God and the salvation of humanity. Incorporated in Jesus Christ, the baptized are united to him and to his sacrifice in the offering they make of themselves and their daily activities (cf. Rom 12:1, 2). Speaking of the lay faithful the Council says: "For their work, prayers and apostolic endeavors, their ordinary married and family life, their daily labor, their mental and physical relaxation, if carried out in the Spirit, and even the hardships of life if patiently borne—all of these become spiritual sacrifices acceptable to God through Jesus Christ (cf. 1 Pt 2:5). During the celebration of the Eucharist these sacrifices are most lovingly offered to the Father along with the Lord's body. Thus as worshipers whose every deed is holy, the lay faithful consecrate the world itself to God."[23]

Through their participation in the *prophetic mission* of Christ, "who proclaimed the kingdom of his Father by the testimony of his life and by the power of his word,"[24] the lay faithful are given the ability and responsibility to accept the Gospel in faith and to proclaim it in word and deed, without hesitating to courageously identify and denounce evil. United to Christ, the "great prophet" (Lk 7:16), and in the Spirit made "witnesses" of the Risen Christ, the lay faithful are made sharers in the appreciation of the Church's supernatural faith, that "cannot err in matters of belief"[25] and sharers as well in the grace of the word (cf. Acts 2:17-18; Rev 19-10). They are also called to allow the newness and the power of the Gospel to shine out everyday in their family and social life, as well as to express patiently and courageously in the contradictions of the present age their hope of future glory even "through the framework of their secular life."[26]

Because the lay faithful belong to Christ, Lord and King of the Universe, they share in his *kingly mission* and are called by him to spread that Kingdom in history. They exercise their kingship as Christians, above all in the spiritual combat in which they seek to overcome in themselves the kingdom of sin (cf. Rom 6:12), and then to make a gift of themselves so as to serve, in justice and in charity, Jesus who is himself present in all his brothers and sisters, above all in the very least (cf. Mt 25:40).

But in particular the lay faithful are called to restore to creation all its original value. In ordering creation to the authentic well-being of humanity in an activity governed by the life of grace, they share in the exercise of the power with which the Risen Christ draws all things to himself and subjects them along with himself to the Father, so that God might be everything to everyone (cf. 1 Cor 15:28; Jn 12:32).

The participation of the lay faithful in the threefold mission of Christ as Priest, Prophet and

King finds its source in the anointing of Baptism, its further development in Confirmation and its realization and dynamic sustenance in the Holy Eucharist. It is a participation given to each member of the lay faithful *individually,* inasmuch as each is one of the *many* who form the *one Body* of the Lord: in fact, Jesus showers his gifts upon the Church which is his Body and his Spouse. In such a way individuals are sharers in the threefold mission of Christ in virtue of their being members of the Church, as St. Peter clearly teaches when he defines the baptized as "a chosen race, a royal priesthood, a holy nation, God's own people" (1 Pt 2:9). Precisely because it derives *from* Church *communion,* the sharing of the lay faithful in the threefold mission of Christ requires that it be lived and realized *in communion* and *for the increase of communion itself.* St. Augustine writes: "As we call everyone 'Christians' in virtue of a mystical anointing, so we call everyone 'priests' because all are members of only one priesthood." [27]

The Lay Faithful and Their Secular Character

15. The newness of the Christian life is the foundation and title for equality among all the baptized in Christ, for all the members of the People of God: "As members, they share a common dignity from their rebirth in Christ, they have the same filial grace and the same vocation to perfection. They possess in common one salvation, one hope and one undivided charity." [28] Because of the one dignity flowing from Baptism, each member of the lay faithful, together with

ordained ministers and men and women religious, shares a responsibility for the Church's mission.

But among the lay faithful this one baptismal dignity takes on *a manner of life which sets a person apart, without, however, bringing about a separation* from the ministerial priesthood or from men and women religious. The Second Vatican Council has described this manner of life as the "secular character": "The secular character is properly and particularly that of the lay faithful." [29]

To understand properly the lay faithful's position in the Church in a complete, adequate and specific manner it is necessary to come to a deeper theological understanding of their secular character in light of God's plan of salvation and in the context of the mystery of the Church.

Pope Paul VI said the Church "has an authentic secular dimension, inherent to her inner nature and mission, which is deeply rooted in the mystery of the Word Incarnate, and which is realized in different forms through her members." [30]

The Church, in fact, lives in the world, even if she is not of the world (cf. Jn 17:16). She is sent to continue the redemptive work of Jesus Christ, which "by its very nature concerns the salvation of humanity, and also involves the renewal of the whole temporal order." [31]

Certainly *all the members* of the Church are sharers in this secular dimension but *in different ways*. In particular the sharing of the *lay faithful* has its own manner of realization and function, which, according to the Council, is "properly and particularly" theirs. Such manner is designated with the expression "secular character." [32]

In fact the Council, in describing the lay faithful's situation in the secular world, points to it above all, as the place in which they receive their call from God: "There they are called by God." [33] This "place" is treated and presented in dynamic terms: the lay faithful "live in the world, that is, in every one of the secular professions and occupations. They live in the ordinary circumstances of family and social life, from which the very fabric of their existence is woven." [34] They are persons who live an ordinary life in the world: they study, they work, they form relationships as friends, professionals, members of society, cultures, etc. However, the Council considers their condition not simply an external and environmental framework, but as a reality *destined to find in Jesus Christ the fullness of its meaning.* [35] Indeed it leads to the affirmation that "the Word made flesh willed to share in human fellowship.... He sanctified those human ties, especially family ones, from which social relationships arise, willingly submitting himself to the laws of his country. He chose to lead the life of an ordinary craftsman of his own time and place." [36]

The "world" thus becomes the place and the means for the lay faithful to fulfill their Christian vocation because the world itself is destined to glorify God the Father in Christ. The Council is able then to indicate the proper and special sense of the divine vocation which is directed to the lay faithful. They are not called to abandon the position that they have in the world. Baptism does not take them from the world at all, as the Apostle Paul points out: "So, brethren, in whatever state each was called, there let him remain with God" (1 Cor 7:24). On the contrary, he entrusts a vocation to them that properly concerns their situation in the world. The lay faithful, in fact, "are called by God so that they, led by the spirit of the Gospel, might contribute to the sanctification of the world, as from within like leaven, by fulfilling their own particular duties. Thus, especially in this way of life, resplendent in faith, hope and charity they manifest Christ to others."[37] Thus for the lay faithful, to be present and active in the world is not only an anthropological and sociological reality, but in a specific way, a theological and ecclesiological reality as well. In fact, in their situation in the world, God manifests his plan and communicates to them their particular vocation of "seeking the Kingdom of God by engaging in temporal affairs and by ordering them according to the plan of God."[38]

Precisely with this in mind the Synod Fathers said: "The secular character of the lay faithful is not therefore to be defined only in a sociological sense, but most especially in a theological sense. The term *secular* must be understood in light of the act of God the creator and redeemer, who has handed over the world to women and men, so that they may participate in the work of creation, free from the influence of sin and sanctify themselves in marriage or the celibate life, in a family, in a profession, and in the various activities of society."[39]

The lay faithful's *position in the Church,* then, comes to be fundamentally defined by their *new-*

ness in Christian life and distinguished by their *secular character.*[40]

The images of salt, light and leaven taken from the Gospel, although indiscriminately applicable to all Jesus' disciples, are specifically applied to the lay faithful. They are particularly meaningful images because they speak not only of the deep involvement and the full participation of the lay faithful in the affairs of the earth, the world and the human community, but also and above all, they tell of the radical newness and unique character of an involvement and participation which has as its purpose the spreading of the Gospel that brings salvation.

Called to Holiness

16. We come to a full sense of the dignity of the lay faithful if we consider *the prime and fundamental vocation* that the Father assigns to each of them in Jesus Christ through the Holy Spirit: the vocation to holiness, that is, the perfection of charity. Holiness is the greatest testimony of the dignity conferred on a disciple of Christ.

The Second Vatican Council has significantly spoken on the universal call to holiness. It is possible to say that this call to holiness is precisely the basic charge entrusted to all the sons and daughters of the Church by a Council which intended to bring a renewal of Christian life based on the Gospel.[41] This charge is not a simple moral exhortation but an *undeniable requirement arising from the mystery of the Church: she is the choice vine* whose branches live and grow with the same holy and life-giving energies that come from

Christ; she is the Mystical Body whose members share in the same life of holiness of the Head who is Christ; she is the Beloved Spouse of the Lord Jesus who delivered himself up for her sanctification (cf. Eph 5:25ff.). The Spirit that sanctified the human nature of Jesus in Mary's virginal womb (cf. Lk 1:35) is the same Spirit that is abiding and working in the Church to communicate to her the holiness of the Son of God made man.

It is ever more urgent that today all Christians take up again the way of the gospel renewal, welcoming in a spirit of generosity the invitation expressed by the Apostle Peter "to be holy in all conduct" (1 Pt 1:15). The 1985 Extraordinary Synod, twenty years after the Council, opportunely insisted on this urgency: "Since the Church in Christ is a mystery, she ought to be considered the sign and instrument of holiness.... Men and women saints have always been the source and origin of renewal in the most difficult circumstances in the Church's history. Today we have the greatest need of saints whom we must assiduously beg God to raise up." [42]

Everyone in the Church, precisely because they are members, receives and thereby shares in the common vocation to holiness. In the fullness of this title and on equal par with all other members of the Church, the lay faithful are called to holiness: "All the faithful of Christ of whatever rank or status are called to the fullness of Christian life and to the perfection of charity"; [43] "All of Christ's followers are invited and bound to pursue holiness and the perfect fulfillment of their own state of life." [44]

The call to holiness is *rooted in Baptism* and proposed anew in the other Sacraments, principally in the *Eucharist*. Since Christians are re-clothed in Christ Jesus and refreshed by his Spirit, they are "holy." They therefore have the ability to manifest this holiness and the responsibility to bear witness to it in all that they do. The Apostle Paul never tires of admonishing all Christians to live "as is fitting among saints" (Eph 5:3).

Life according to the Spirit, whose fruit is holiness (cf. Rom 6:22; Gal 5:22), stirs up every baptized person and requires each to *follow and imitate Jesus Christ* in embracing the Beatitudes; in listening and meditating on the Word of God; in conscious and active participation in the liturgical and sacramental life of the Church; in personal prayer; in family or in community; in the hunger and thirst for justice; in the practice of the commandment of love in all circumstances of life and service to the brethren, especially the least, the poor and the suffering.

The Life of Holiness in the World

17. The vocation of the lay faithful to holiness implies that life according to the Spirit expresses itself in a particular way in their *involvement in temporal affairs* and in their *participation in earthly activities*. Once again the Apostle admonishes us: "Whatever you do, in word or deed, do everything in the name of the Lord Jesus, giving thanks to God the Father through him" (1 Col 3:17). Applying the Apostle's words to the

lay faithful, the Council categorically affirms: "Neither family concerns nor other secular affairs should be excluded from their religious program of life." [45] Likewise the Synod Fathers have said: "The unity of life of the lay faithful is of the greatest importance: indeed they must be sanctified in everyday professional and social life. Therefore, to respond to their vocation, the lay faithful must see their daily activities as an occasion to join themselves to God, fulfill his will, serve other people and lead them to communion with God in Christ." [46]

The vocation to holiness must be recognized and lived by the lay faithful, first of all as an undeniable and demanding obligation and as a shining example of the infinite love of the Father that has regenerated them in his own life of holiness. Such a vocation, then, ought to be called an *essential and inseparable element of the new life of Baptism,* and therefore an element which determines their dignity. At the same time the vocation to holiness is *intimately connected to mission* and to the responsibility entrusted to the lay faithful in the Church and in the world. In fact, that same holiness which is derived simply from their participation in the Church's holiness, represents their first and fundamental contribution to the building of the Church herself, who is the "Communion of Saints." The eyes of faith behold a wonderful scene: that of a countless number of lay people, both women and men, busy at work in their daily life and activity, oftentimes far from view and quite unacclaimed by the world, unknown to the world's great personages but nonetheless looked upon in love by the Father, untiring laborers who work in the Lord's vineyard. Confident and steadfast through the power of God's grace, these are the humble yet great builders of the Kingdom of God in history.

Holiness, then, must be called a fundamental presupposition and an irreplaceable condition for everyone in fulfilling the mission of salvation within the Church. The Church's holiness is the hidden source and the infallible measure of the works of the apostolate and of the missionary effort. Only in the measure that the Church, Christ's Spouse, is loved by him and she, in turn, loves him, does she become a mother fruitful in the Spirit.

Again we take up the image from the Gospel: the fruitfulness and the growth of the branches depends on their remaining united to the vine. "As the branch cannot bear fruit by itself, unless it abides in the vine, neither can you, unless you abide in me. I am the vine, you are the branches. He who abides in me, and I in him, he it is that bears much fruit, for apart from me you can do nothing" (Jn 15:4-5).

It is appropriate to recall here the solemn proclamation of beatification and canonization of lay men and women which took place during the month of the Synod. The entire People of God, and the lay faithful in particular, can find at this moment new models of holiness and new witnesses of heroic virtue lived in the ordinary everyday circumstances of human existence. The Synod Fathers have said: "Particular Churches especially should be attentive to recognizing among their members the younger men and women of those Churches who have given witness to holiness in such conditions [everyday secular conditions and the conjugal state] and who can be an example for others, so that, if the case calls for it, they [the Churches] might propose them to be beatified and canonized." [47]

At the end of these reflections intended to define the lay faithful's position in the Church, the celebrated admonition of St. Leo the Great comes to mind: "Acknowledge, O Christian, your dignity!" [48] St. Maximus, Bishop of Turin, in addressing those who had received the holy anointing of Baptism, repeats the same sentiments: "Ponder the honor that has made you sharers in this mystery!" [49] All the baptized are invited to hear once again the words of St. Augustine: "Let us rejoice and give thanks; we have not only become Christians, but Christ himself.... Stand in awe and rejoice, we have become Christ." [50]

The dignity as a Christian, the source of equality for all members of the Church, guarantees and fosters the spirit of *communion* and fellowship, and, at the same time, becomes the hidden dynamic force in the lay faithful's apostolate and mission. It is a *dignity,* however, *which brings demands,* the dignity of laborers called by the Lord to work in his vineyard: "Upon all the lay faithful, then, rests the exalted duty of working to assure that each day the divine plan of salvation is further extended to every person, of every era, in every part of the earth." [51]

II
All Branches of a Single Vine

The Participation of the Lay Faithful
in the Life of Church as Communion

The Mystery of Church Communion

18. Again we turn to the words of Jesus: "I am the true vine and my Father is the vine-dresser.... *Abide in me and I in you*" (Jn 15:1, 4).

These simple words reveal the mystery of communion that serves as the unifying bond between the Lord and his disciples, between Christ and the baptized—a living and life-giving communion through which Christians no longer belong to themselves but are the Lord's very own, as the branches are one with the vine.

The communion of Christians with Jesus has the communion of God as Trinity, namely, the unity of the Son to the Father in the gift of the Holy Spirit, as its model and source, and is itself the means to achieve this communion: united to the Son in the Spirit's bond of love, Christians are united to the Father.

Jesus continues: *"I am the vine, you are the branches"* (Jn 15:5). From the communion that Christians experience in Christ there immediately flows the communion which they experience with one another: all are branches of a single vine, namely, Christ. In this communion is the wonderful reflection and participation in the mystery of the intimate life of love in God as Trinity, Father, Son and Holy Spirit as revealed by the Lord Jesus. For this *communion* Jesus prays: "that they may all be one; even as you, Father, are in me, and I in you, that they also may be in us, so that the world may believe that you have sent me" (Jn 17:21).

Such communion is the very mystery of the Church, as the Second Vatican Council recalls in the celebrated words of St. Cyprian: "The Church shines forth as 'a people made one with the unity of the Father, Son and Holy Spirit.'"[52] We are accustomed to recall this mystery of Church *communion* at the beginning of the celebration of the Eucharist when the priest welcomes all with the greeting of the Apostle Paul: "The grace of the Lord Jesus, the love of God and the fellowship of the Holy Spirit be with you all" (2 Cor 13:13).

After having described the distinguishing features of the lay faithful on which their dignity rests, we must at this moment reflect on their mission and responsibility in the Church and in the world. A proper understanding of these aspects, however, can be found only in the living context of the Church as *communion*.

Vatican II
and the Ecclesiology of Communion

19. At the Second Vatican Council the Church again proposed this central idea about herself, as the 1985 Extraordinary Synod recalls: "The eccle-

siology of *communion* is a central and fundamental concept in the conciliar documents. *Koinonia-communion,* finding its source in Sacred Scripture, was a concept held in great honor in the early Church and in the Oriental Churches, and this teaching endures to the present day. Much was done by the Second Vatican Council to bring about a clearer understanding of the Church as *communion* and its concrete application to life. What, then, does this complex word *'communion'* mean? Its fundamental meaning speaks of the union with God brought about by Jesus Christ, in the Holy Spirit. The opportunity for such *communion* is present in the Word of God and in the Sacraments. Baptism is the door and the foundation of *communion* in the Church. The Eucharist is the source and summit of the whole Christian life (cf. *Lumen Gentium,* 11). The Body of Christ in the Holy Eucharist sacramentalizes this communion, that is, it is a sign and actually brings about the intimate bonds of *communion* among all the faithful in the Body of Christ which is the Church (1 Cor 10:16)." [53]

On the day after the conclusion of the Council Pope Paul VI addressed the faithful in the following words: "The Church is a *communion.* In this context what does *communion* mean? We refer to the paragraph in the Catechism that speaks of the *sanctorum communionem,* 'the Communion of Saints.' The meaning of the Church is a communion of saints. 'Communion' speaks of a double, life-giving participation: the incorporation of Christians into the life of Christ, and the communication of that life of charity to the entire body of the Faithful, in this world and in the next, union with Christ and in Christ, and union among Christians, in the Church."[54]

Vatican Council II has invited us to contemplate the mystery of the Church through biblical images which bring to light the reality of the Church as a *communion* with its inseparable dimensions: the communion of each Christian with Christ and the communion of all Christians with one another. There is the sheepfold, the flock, the vine, the spiritual building, the Holy City.[55] Above all, there is the image of the *Body* as set forth by the Apostle Paul. Its doctrine finds a pleasing expression once again in various passages of the Council's documents.[56] In its turn, the Council has looked again at the entire history of salvation and has reproposed the image of the Church as the *People of God:* "It has pleased God to make people holy and to save them, not merely as individuals without any mutual bonds, but by making them into a single people, a people which acknowledges him in truth and serves him in holiness."[57] From its opening lines, the Constitution *Lumen Gentium* summarizes this doctrine in a wonderful way: "The Church in Christ is a kind of sacrament, that is, a sign and instrument of intimate union with God and of the unity of all the human race."[58]

The reality of the Church as Communion is, then, the integrating aspect, indeed *the central content of the "mystery,"* or rather, the divine plan for the salvation of humanity. For this purpose ecclesial communion cannot be interpreted in a sufficient way if it is understood as simply a sociological or a psychological reality. The Church as *Communion* is the "new" People, the "messianic" People, the People that "has for its head, Christ... as its heritage, the dignity and freedom of God's Children...for its law, the new commandment to love as Christ loved us...for its goal, the Kingdom of God...established by Christ as a communion of life, love and truth." [59] The bonds that unite the members of the New People among themselves— and first of all with Christ—are not those of "flesh and blood," but those of the spirit, more precisely those of the Holy Spirit, whom all the baptized have received (cf. Joel 3:1).

In fact, that Spirit is the One who from eternity unites the one and undivided Trinity, that Spirit who "in the fullness of time" (Gal 4:4) forever unites human nature to the Son of God, that same identical Spirit who in the course of Christian generations is the constant and never-ending source of communion in the Church.

An Organic Communion: Diversity and Complementarity

20. Ecclesial communion is more precisely likened to an "organic" communion, analogous to that of a living and functioning body. In fact, at one and the same time it is characterized by a *diversity* and a *complementarity* of vocations and states in life, of ministries, of charisms and responsibilities. Because of this diversity and complementarity every member of the lay faithful is seen *in relation to the whole body* and offers a *totally unique contribution* on behalf of the whole body.

St. Paul insists in a particular way on the organic communion of the Mystical Body of Christ. We can hear his rich teaching echoed in the following synthesis from the Council: "Jesus Christ"—we read in the Constitution *Lumen Gentium*—"by communicating his spirit to his brothers and sisters, called together from all peoples, made them mystically into his own body. In that body, the life of Christ is communicated to those who believe.... As all the members of the human body, though they are many, form one body, so also are the Faithful in Christ (cf. 1 Cor 12:12). Also, in the building up of Christ's body there is a diversity of members and functions. There is only one Spirit who, according to his own richness and the necessities of service, distributes his different gifts for the welfare of the Church (cf. 1 Cor 12:1-11). Among these gifts comes in the first place the grace given to the apostles to whose authority the Spirit himself subjects even those who are endowed with charisms (cf. 1 Cor 14). Furthermore it is this same Spirit, who through his power and through the intimate bond between the members, produces and urges love among the faithful. Consequently, if one member suffers anything, all the members suffer it too, and if one member is honored, all members together rejoice" (cf. 1 Cor 12:26).[60]

One and the same Spirit is always the dynamic principle of diversity and unity in the Church. Once again we read in the Constitution *Lumen Gentium,* "In order that we might be unceasingly renewed in him (cf. Eph 4:23), he has shared with us his Spirit who, existing as one and the same being in the head and in the members, gives life to, unifies and moves the whole body. This he does in such a way that his work could be compared by the Fathers to the function which the soul as the principle of life fulfills in the human body." [61] And in another particularly significant text which is helpful in understanding not only the organic nature proper to ecclesial communion but also its aspect of growth towards perfect communion, the Council writes: "The Spirit dwells in the Church and in the hearts of the Faithful, as in a temple (cf. 1 Cor 3:16; 6:19). In them he prays and bears witness that they are adopted sons (cf. Gal 4:6; Rom 8:15-16, 26). Guiding the Church in the way of all truth (cf. Jn 16:13) and unifying her in communion and in the works of service, he bestows upon her varied hierarchical and charismatic gifts and adorns her with the fruits of his grace (cf. Eph 4:11-12; 1 Cor 12:4; Gal 5:22). By the power of the Gospel he makes the Church grow, perpetually renews her, and leads her to perfect union with her Spouse. The Spirit and the Bride both say to the Lord Jesus, 'Come!' (cf. Rev 22:17)." [62]

Church communion then is a gift, a great gift of the Holy Spirit to be gratefully accepted by the lay faithful, and at the same time to be lived with a deep sense of responsibility. This is concretely realized through their participation in the life and mission of the Church, to whose service the lay faithful put their varied and complementary ministries and charisms.

A member of the lay faithful "can never remain in isolation from the community, but must live in a continual interaction with others, with a lively sense of fellowship, rejoicing in an equal dignity and common commitment to bring to fruition the immense treasure that each has inherited. The Spirit of the Lord gives a vast variety of charisms, inviting people to assume different ministries and forms of service and reminding them, as he reminds all people in their relationship in the Church, that what distinguishes persons is *not an increase in dignity,* but *a special and complementary capacity for service....* Thus, the charisms, the ministries, the different forms of service exercised by the lay faithful exist in communion and on behalf of communion. They are treasures that complement one another for the good of all and are under the wise guidance of their Pastors." [63]

Ministries and Charisms:
The Spirit's Gifts to the Church

21. The Second Vatican Council speaks of the ministries and charisms as the gifts of the Holy Spirit which are given for the building up of the Body of Christ and for its mission of salvation in the world.[64] Indeed, the Church is directed and guided by the Holy Spirit, who lavishes diverse hierarchical and charismatic gifts on all the baptized, calling them to be, each in an individual way, active and co-responsible.

We now turn our thoughts to ministries and charisms as they directly relate to the lay faithful and to their participation in the life of Church-Communion.

Ministries, Offices and Roles

The ministries which exist and are at work at this time in the Church are all—even in their variety of forms—a participation in Jesus Christ's own ministry as the Good Shepherd who lays down his life for the sheep (cf. Jn 10:11), the humble servant who gives himself without reserve for the salvation of all (cf. Mk 10:45). The Apostle Paul is quite clear in speaking about the ministerial constitution of the Church in apostolic times. In his First Letter to the Corinthians he writes: "And God has appointed in the Church first apostles, second prophets, third teachers..." (1 Cor 12:28). In his Letter to the Ephesians we read: "But the grace was given to each of us according to the measure of Christ's gift.... And his gifts were that some should be apostles, some prophets, some evangelists, some pastors and teachers, to equip the saints for the work of ministry, for building up the body of Christ until we all attain to the unity of the faith and of the knowledge of the Son of God, to mature manhood, to the measure of the stature of the fullness of Christ" (Eph 4:7, 11-13; cf. Rom 12:4-8). These and other New Testament texts indicate the diversity of ministries as well as of gifts and ecclesial tasks.

The Ministries
Derived from Holy Orders

22. In a primary position in the Church are the *ordained ministries,* that is, the ministries *that come from the Sacrament of Orders.* In fact, with the mandate to make disciples of all nations (cf.

Mt 28:19), the Lord Jesus chose and constituted the apostles—seed of the People of the New Covenant and origin of the Hierarchy[65]—to form and to rule the priestly people. The mission of the Apostles, which the Lord Jesus continues to entrust to the pastors of his people, is a true service, significantly referred to in Sacred Scripture as *"diakonia,"* namely, service or ministry. The ministries receive the charism of the Holy Spirit from the Risen Christ in uninterrupted succession from the apostles, through the Sacrament of Orders. From him they receive the authority and sacred power to serve the Church, acting *in persona Christi Capitas* (in the person of Christ, the Head)[66] and to gather her in the Holy Spirit through the Gospel and the Sacraments.

The ordained ministries, apart from the persons who receive them, are a grace for the entire Church. These ministries express and realize a participation in the priesthood of Jesus Christ that is different, not simply in degree but in essence, from the participation given to all the lay faithful through Baptism and Confirmation. On the other hand, the ministerial priesthood, as the Second Vatican Council recalls, essentially has the royal priesthood of all the faithful as its aim and is ordered to it.[67]

For this reason, so as to assure and to increase communion in the Church, particularly in those places where there is a diversity and complementarity of ministries, pastors must always acknowledge that their ministry is fundamentally ordered to the service of the entire People of God (cf. Heb 5:1). The lay faithful, in turn, must acknowledge that the ministerial priesthood is totally necessary for their participation in the mission in the Church.[68]

The Ministries,
Offices and Roles of the Lay Faithful

23. The Church's mission of salvation in the world is realized not only by the ministers in virtue of the Sacrament of Orders but also by all the lay faithful; indeed, because of their Baptismal state and their specific vocation, in the measure proper to each person, the lay faithful participate in the priestly, prophetic and kingly mission of Christ.

The pastors, therefore, ought to acknowledge and foster the ministries, the offices and roles of the lay faithful that find their *foundation in the Sacraments of Baptism and Confirmation*, indeed, for a good many of them, *in the Sacrament of Matrimony*.

When necessity and expediency in the Church require it, the pastors, according to established norms from universal law, can entrust to the lay faithful certain offices and roles that are connected to their pastoral ministry but do not require the character of Orders. The Code of Canon Law states: "When the necessity of the Church warrants it and when ministers are lacking, lay persons, even if they are not lectors or acolytes, can also supply for certain of their offices, namely, to exercise the ministry of the word, to preside over liturgical prayers, to confer Baptism, and to distribute Holy Communion in accord with the prescriptions of the law."[69] However, *the exercise* of such tasks does not make the lay faithful pastors: in fact, a person is not a minister simply in performing a task, but through sacramental ordination. Only the Sacrament of Orders gives the ordained minister a particular participation in the office of Christ, the Shepherd and Head, and in his Eternal Priesthood.[70] The task exercised in virtue of supply takes its legitimacy formally and immediately from the official deputation given by the pastors, as well as from its concrete exercise under the guidance of ecclesiastical authority.[71]

The recent Synodal Assembly has provided an extensive and meaningful overview of the situation in the Church on the ministries, offices and roles of the baptized. The Fathers have manifested a deep appreciation for the contribution of the lay faithful, both women and men, in the work of the apostolate, in evangelization, sanctification and the Christian animation of temporal affairs, as well as their generous willingness to supply in situations of emergency and chronic necessity.[72]

Following the liturgical renewal promoted by the Council, the lay faithful themselves have acquired a more lively awareness of the tasks that they fulfill in the liturgical assembly and its preparation, and have become more widely disposed to fulfill them: the liturgical celebration, in fact, is a sacred action not simply of the clergy, but of the entire assembly. It is, therefore, natural that the tasks not proper to the ordained ministers be fulfilled by the lay faithful.[73] In this way there is a natural transition from an effective involvement of the lay faithful in the liturgical action to that of announcing the word of God and pastoral care.[74]

In the same Synod Assembly, however, a critical judgment was voiced along with these positive elements, about a too-indiscriminate use of the word "ministry," the confusion and the equating of the common priesthood and the ministerial priesthood, the lack of observance of ecclesiastical laws and norms, the arbitrary interpretation of the concept of "supply," the tendency towards a "clericalization" of the lay faithful and the risk of creating, in reality, an ecclesial structure of parallel service to that founded on the Sacrament of Orders.

Precisely to overcome these dangers the Synod Fathers have insisted on the necessity to express with greater clarity, and with a more precise terminology,[75] both *the unity of the Church's mission* in which all the baptized participate, and the substantial *diversity of the ministry* of pastors which is rooted in the Sacrament of Orders, all the while respecting the other ministries, offices and roles in the Church, which are rooted in the Sacraments of Baptism and Confirmation.

In the first place, then, it is necessary that in acknowledging and in conferring various ministries, offices and roles on the lay faithful, the pastors exercise the maximum care to institute them on the basis of Baptism in which these tasks are rooted. It is also necessary that pastors guard against a facile yet abusive recourse to a presumed "situation of emergency" or to "supply by necessity," where objectively this does not exist or where alternative possibilities could exist through better pastoral planning.

The various ministries, offices and roles that

the lay faithful can legitimately fulfill in the liturgy, in the transmission of the faith, and in the pastoral structure of the Church, ought to be exercised *in conformity to their specific lay vocation* which is different from that of the sacred ministry. In this regard the Exhortation *Evangelii Nuntiandi,* that had such a great part in stimulating the varied collaboration of the lay faithful in the Church's life and mission of spreading the Gospel, recalls that "their own field of evangelizing activity is the vast and complicated world of politics, society and economics, as well as the world of culture, of the sciences and the arts, of international life, of the mass media. It also includes other realities which are open to evangelization, such as human love, the family, the education of children and adolescents, professional work, and suffering. The more Gospel-inspired lay people there are engaged in these realities, clearly involved in them, competent to promote them, and conscious that they must exercise to the full their Christian powers which are often repressed and buried, the more these realities will be at the service of the Kingdom of God and therefore at the service of salvation in Jesus Christ, without in any way losing or sacrificing their human content but rather pointing to a transcendent dimension which is often disregarded." [76]

In the course of Synod work the Fathers devoted much attention to the *Lectorate* and the *Acolytate.* While in the past these ministries existed in the Latin Church only as spiritual steps on route to the ordained ministry, with the *motu proprio* of Paul VI, *Ministeria Quaedam* (August 15,

1972), they assumed an autonomy and stability, as well as a possibility of their being given to the lay faithful, albeit, only to men. The same fact is expressed in the new Code of Canon Law.[77] At this time the Synod Fathers expressed the desire that "the *motu proprio Ministeria Quaedam* be reconsidered, bearing in mind the present practice of local churches and above all indicating criteria which ought to be used in choosing those destined for each ministry."[78]

In this regard a Commission was established to respond to this desire voiced by the Synod Fathers, specifically to provide an in-depth study of the various theological, liturgical, juridical and pastoral considerations which are associated with the great increase today of the ministries entrusted to the lay faithful.

While the conclusions of the Commission's study are awaited, a more ordered and fruitful ecclesial practice of the ministries entrusted to the lay faithful can be achieved if all the particular Churches faithfully respect the above mentioned theological principles, especially the essential difference between the ministerial priesthood and the common priesthood, and the difference between the ministries derived from the Sacrament of Orders and those derived from the Sacraments of Baptism and Confirmation.

Charisms

24. The Holy Spirit, while bestowing diverse ministries in Church communion, enriches it still further with particular gifts or promptings of grace, called *charisms*. These can take a great

variety of forms both as a manifestation of the absolute freedom of the Spirit who abundantly supplies them, and as a response to the varied needs of the Church in history. The description and the classification given to these gifts in the New Testament are an indication of their rich variety. "To each is given the manifestation of the Spirit for the common good. To one is given through the Spirit the utterance of wisdom, and to another the utterance of knowledge according to the same Spirit, to another faith by the same Spirit, to another gifts of healing by the one Spirit, to another the working of miracles, to another prophecy, to another the ability to distinguish between spirits, to another various kinds of tongues, to another the interpretation of tongues" (1 Cor 12:7-10; cf. 1 Cor 12:4-6, 28-31; Rom 12:6-8; 1 Pt 4:10-11).

Whether they be exceptional and great or simple and ordinary, the charisms are *graces of the Holy Spirit that have,* directly or indirectly, *a usefulness for the ecclesial community,* ordered as they are to the building up of the Church, to the well-being of humanity and to the needs of the world.

Even in our own times there is no lack of a fruitful manifestation of various charisms among the faithful, women and men. These charisms are given to individual persons and can even be shared by others in such ways as to continue in time a precious and effective heritage, serving as a source of a particular spiritual affinity among persons. In referring to the apostolate of the lay faithful the Second Vatican Council writes: "For the exercise of the apostolate the Holy Spirit who sanctifies the People of God through the ministry and the sacraments gives the faithful special gifts as well (cf. 1 Cor 12:7), 'allotting them to each one as he wills' (cf. 1 Cor 12:11), so that each might place 'at the service of others the grace received' and become 'good stewards of God's varied grace' (1 Pt 4:10), and build up thereby the whole body in charity (cf. Eph 4:16)." [79]

By a logic which looks to the divine source of this giving, as the Council recalls, [80] the gifts of the Spirit demand that those who have received them exercise them for the growth of the whole Church.

The charisms are *received in gratitude* both on the part of the one who receives them, and also on the part of the entire Church. They are in fact a singularly rich source of grace for the vitality of the apostolate and for the holiness of the whole Body of Christ, provided that they be gifts that come truly from the Spirit and are exercised in full conformity with the authentic promptings of the Spirit. In this sense the *discernment of charisms* is always necessary. Indeed, the Synod Fathers have stated: "The action of the Holy Spirit, who breathes where he will, is not always easily recognized and received. We know that God acts in all Christians, and we are aware of the benefits which flow from charisms both for individuals and for the whole Christian community. Nevertheless, at the same time we are also aware of the power of sin and how it can disturb and confuse the life of the faithful and of the community." [81]

For this reason no charism dispenses a person from reference and submission to the *Pastors of the Church.* The Council clearly states: "Judgment as to their [charisms'] genuineness and proper use belongs to those who preside over the Church, and to whose special competence it belongs, not indeed to extinguish the Spirit, but to test all things and hold fast to what is good (cf. 1 Thes 5:12 and 19-21)," [82] so that all the charisms might work together, in their diversity and complementarity, for the common good. [83]

The Lay Faithful's Participation in the Life of the Church

25. The lay faithful participate in the life of the Church not only in exercising their tasks and charisms, but also in many other ways.

Such participation finds its first and necessary expression in the life and mission of the *particular Church,* in the diocese in which "the Church of Christ, one, holy, catholic and apostolic, is truly present and at work." [84]

The Particular Churches and the Universal Church

For an adequate participation in ecclesial life the lay faithful absolutely need to have a clear and precise vision of the *particular Church with its primordial bond to the universal Church.* The particular Church does not come about from a kind of fragmentation of the universal Church, nor does the universal Church come about by a simple amalgamation of particular Churches. Rather, there is a real, essential and constant bond uniting each of them and this is why the universal Church exists and is manifested in the particular

Churches. For this reason the Council says that the particular Churches "are constituted after the model of the universal Church; it is in and from these particular Churches that there come into being the one and unique Catholic Church."[85]

The same Council strongly encourages the lay faithful to live out actively their belonging to the particular Church, while at the same time assuming an ever-increasing "catholic" spirit: "Let the lay faithful constantly foster"—we read in the Decree on the Apostolate of Lay People—"a feeling for their own diocese, of which the parish is a kind of cell, and be always ready at their bishops' invitation to participate in diocesan projects. Indeed, if the needs of cities and rural areas are to be met, lay people should not limit their cooperation to the parochial or diocesan boundaries, but strive to extend it to interparochial, interdiocesan, national and international fields—more so because the daily increase in population mobility, the growth of mutual bonds, and the ease of communication no longer allow any sector of society to remain closed in upon itself. Thus they should be concerned about the needs of the People of God scattered throughout the world."[86]

In this sense, the recent Synod has favored the creation of *Diocesan Pastoral Councils* as a recourse at opportune times. In fact, on a diocesan level this structure could be the principle form of collaboration, dialogue, and discernment as well. The participation of the lay faithful in these Councils can broaden resources in consultation and the principle of collaboration—and in certain instances also in decision-making—if applied in a broad and determined manner.[87]

The participation of the lay faithful in *Diocesan Synods* and in *Local Councils,* whether provincial or plenary, is envisioned by the Code of Canon Law.[88] These structures could contribute to Church communion and the mission of the particular Church, both in its own surroundings and in relation to the other particular Churches of the ecclesiastical province or Episcopal Conference.

Episcopal Conferences are called to evaluate the most opportune way of developing the consultation and the collaboration of the lay faithful, women and men, at a national or regional level, so that they may consider well the problems they share and manifest better the communion of the whole Church.[89]

The Parish

26. The ecclesial community, while always having a universal dimension, finds its most immediate and visible expression in the *parish*. It is there that the Church is seen locally. In a certain sense it is the *Church living in the midst of the homes of her sons and daughters.*[90]

It is necessary that in light of the faith all rediscover the true meaning of the parish, that is, the place where the very "mystery" of the Church is present and at work, even if at times it is lacking persons and means, even if at other times it might be scattered over vast territories or almost not to be found in crowded and chaotic modern sections of cities. The parish is not principally a structure, a territory, or a building, but rather, "the family of

God, a fellowship afire with a unifying spirit,"[91] "a familial and welcoming home,"[92] the "community of the faithful."[93] Plainly and simply, the parish is founded on a theological reality because it is a *Eucharistic community.*[94] This means that the parish is a community properly suited for celebrating the Eucharist, the living source for its upbuilding and the sacramental bond of its being in full communion with the whole Church. Such suitableness is rooted in the fact that the parish is a *community of faith* and an *organic community,* that is, constituted by the ordained ministers and other Christians, in which the pastor—who represents the diocesan bishop[95]—is the hierarchical bond with the entire particular Church.

Since the Church's task in our day is so great, its accomplishment cannot be left to the parish alone. For this reason the Code of Canon Law provides for forms of collaboration among parishes in a given territory[96] and recommends to the bishop's care the various groups of the Christian Faithful, even the unbaptized who are not under his ordinary pastoral care.[97] There are many other places and forms of association through which the Church can be present and at work. All are necessary to carry out the word and grace of the Gospel and to correspond to the various circumstances of life in which people find themselves today. In a similar way there exist in the areas of culture, society, education, professions, etc., many other ways for spreading the faith and other settings for the apostolate which cannot have the parish as their center and origin. Nevertheless, in our day the parish still enjoys a new and promising season.

At the beginning of his pontificate, Paul VI addressed the Roman clergy in these words: "We believe simply that this old and venerable structure of the parish has an indispensable mission of great contemporary importance: to create the basic community of the Christian people; to initiate and gather the people in the accustomed expression of liturgical life; to conserve and renew the faith in the people of today; to serve as the school for teaching the salvific message of Christ; to put solidarity in practice and work the humble charity of good and brotherly works."[98]

The Synod Fathers for their part have given much attention to the present state of many parishes and have called for a *greater effort in their renewal:* "Many parishes, whether established in regions affected by urban progress or in missionary territory, cannot do their work effectively because they lack material resources or ordained men or are too big geographically or because of the particular circumstances of some Christians (e.g., exiles and migrants). So that all parishes of this kind may be truly communities of Christians, local ecclesial authorities ought to foster the following: a) adaptation of parish structures according to the full flexibility granted by canon law, especially in promoting participation by the lay faithful in pastoral responsibilities; b) small, basic or so-called "living" communities, where the faithful can communicate the Word of God and express it in service and love to one another; these communities are true expressions of ecclesial communion and centers of evangelization, in communion with their pastors."[99] For the renewal of parishes and for a better assurance of their effectiveness in work, various forms of cooperation even on the institutional level ought to be fostered among diverse parishes in the same area.

The Apostolic Commitment in the Parish

27. It is now necessary to look more closely at the communion and participation of the lay faithful in parish life. In this regard all lay men and women are called to give greater attention to a particularly meaningful, stirring and incisive passage from the Council: "Their activity within Church communities is so necessary that without it the apostolate of the pastors is generally unable to achieve its full effectiveness."[100]

This is indeed a particularly important affirmation which evidently must be interpreted in light of the "ecclesiology of communion." Ministries and charisms, being diverse and complementary, are—each in their own way—all necessary for the Church to grow.

The lay faithful ought to be ever more convinced of the special meaning that their commitment to the apostolate takes on in their parish. Once again the Council authoritatively places it in relief: "The parish offers an outstanding example of the apostolate on the community level inasmuch as it brings together the many human differences found within its boundaries, and draws them into the universality of the Church. The lay faithful should accustom themselves to working in the parish in close union with their priests, bringing to the Church community their own and the world's problems as well as questions concerning human salvation—all of which need to be examined to-gether and solved through general discussion. As far as possible the lay faithful ought to collaborate in every apostolic and missionary undertaking sponsored by their own ecclesial family."[101]

The Council's mention of examining and solv-ing pastoral problems "by general discussion" ought to find its adequate and structured develop-ment through a more convinced, extensive and decided appreciation for "Parish Pastoral Coun-cils," on which the Synod Fathers have rightly insisted.[102]

In the present circumstances the lay faithful have the ability to do very much and, therefore, ought to do very much towards the growth of an authentic ecclesial communion in their parishes in order to reawaken missionary zeal towards non-believers and believers themselves who have aban-doned the faith or grown lax in the Christian life.

If indeed, the parish is the Church placed in the neighborhoods of humanity, it lives and is at work through being deeply inserted in human soci-ety and intimately bound up with its aspirations and its dramatic events. Oftentimes the social con-text, especially in certain countries and environ-ments, is violently shaken by elements of disintegration and de-humanization. The individ-ual is lost and disoriented, but there always re-mains in the human heart the desire to experience and cultivate caring and personal relationships. The response to such a desire can come from the parish, when, with the lay faithful's participation, it adheres to its fundamental vocation and mission, that is, to be a "place" in the world for the community of believers to gather together as a "sign" and "instrument" of the vocation of all to communion: in a word, to be a house of welcome to all and a place of service to all, or, as Pope John XXIII was fond of saying, to be the "village fountain" to which all would have recourse in their thirst.

The Forms of Participation in the Life of the Church

28. The lay faithful, together with the clergy and women and men religious, make up the one People of God and the Body of Christ.

Being "members" of the Church takes nothing away from the fact that each Christian as an individual is "unique and irrepeatable." On the contrary, this belonging guarantees and fosters the profound sense of that uniqueness and irrepeatability insofar as these very qualities are the source of variety and richness for the whole Church. Therefore, God calls the individual in Jesus Christ, each one personally by name. In this sense the Lord's words "You too go into my vineyard," directed to the Church as a whole, come specially addressed to each member individually.

Because of each member's unique and irrepeatable character—that is, one's identity and actions as a person—each individual is placed at the service of the growth of the ecclesial community while, at the same time, singularly receiving and sharing in the common richness of all the Church. This is the "Communion of Saints" which we profess in the Creed. *The good of all becomes the good of each one and the good of each one becomes the good of all.* "In the Holy Church," writes St. Gregory the Great, "all are nourished by each one and each one is nourished by all."[103]

Individual Forms of Participation

Above all, each member of the lay faithful should always be *fully aware of being a "member of the Church"* yet entrusted with a unique task which cannot be done by another and which is to be fulfilled for the good of all. From this perspective the Council's insistence on the *absolute necessity of an apostolate exercised by the individual* takes on its full meaning: "The apostolate exercised by the individual—which flows abundantly from a truly Christian life (cf. Jn 4:11)—is the origin and condition of the whole lay apostolate, even in its organized expression, and admits no substitute. Regardless of circumstance, all lay persons (including those who have no opportunity or possibility for collaboration in associations) are called to this type of apostolate and obliged to engage in it. Such an apostolate is useful at all times and places, but in certain circumstances it is the only one available and feasible."[104]

In the apostolate exercised by the individual, great riches are waiting to be discovered through an intensification of the missionary effort of each of the lay faithful. Such an individual form of apostolate can contribute greatly to a *more extensive* spreading of the Gospel, indeed it can reach as many places as there are daily lives of individual members of the lay faithful. Furthermore, the spread of the Gospel will be *continual,* since a person's life and faith will be one. Likewise the spread of the Gospel will be particularly *incisive,* because in sharing fully in the unique conditions of the life, work, difficulties and hopes of their sisters and brothers, the lay faithful will be able to reach the hearts of their neighbors, friends, and colleagues, opening them to a full sense of human existence, that is, to communion with God and with all people.

Group Forms of Participation

29. Church communion, already present and at work in the activities of the individual, finds its specific expression in the lay faithful's working together in groups, that is, in activities done with others in the course of their responsible participation in the life and mission of the Church.

In recent days the phenomenon of lay people associating among themselves has taken on a character of particular variety and vitality. In some ways lay associations have always been present throughout the Church's history as various confraternities, third orders and sodalities testify even today. However, in modern times such lay groups have received a special stimulus, resulting in the birth and spread of a multiplicity of group forms: associations, groups, communities, movements. We can speak of *a new era of group endeavors* of the lay faithful. In fact, "alongside the traditional forming of associations, and at times coming from their very roots, movements and new sodalities have sprouted with a specific feature and purpose, so great is the richness and the versatility of resources that the Holy Spirit nourishes in the ecclesial community, and so great is the capacity of initiative and the generosity of our lay people."[105]

Oftentimes these lay groups show themselves to be *very diverse* from one another in various aspects, in their external structures, in their procedures and training methods, and in the fields in which they work. However, they all come together in an all-inclusive and *profound convergence* when viewed from the perspective of their common purpose, that is, the responsible participation of all of them in the Church's mission of carrying forth the Gospel of Christ—the source of hope for humanity and the renewal of society.

The actual formation of groups of the lay faithful for spiritual purposes or for apostolic work comes from various sources and corresponds to different demands. In fact, their formation itself expresses the social nature of the person and for this reason leads to a more extensive and incisive effectiveness in work. In reality, a "cultural" effect can be accomplished through work done not so much by an individual alone but by an individual as "a social being," that is, as a member of a group, of a community, of an association or of a movement. Such work is, then, the source and stimulus leading to the transformation of the surroundings and society as well as the fruit and sign of every other transformation in this regard. This is particularly true in the context of a pluralistic and fragmented society—the case in so many parts of the world today—and in light of the problems which have become greatly complex and difficult. On the other hand, in a secularized world, above all, the various group forms of the apostolate can represent for many a precious help for the Christian life in remaining faithful to the demands of the Gospel and to the commitment to the Church's mission and the apostolate.

Beyond this, the profound reason that justifies and demands the lay faithful's forming of lay groups comes from a theology *based on ecclesiology,* as the Second Vatican Council clearly acknowledged in referring to the group apostolate as a "sign of communion and of unity of the Church of Christ."[106]

It is a "sign" that must be manifested in relation to "communion" both in the internal and external aspects of the various group forms and in the wider context of the Christian community. As mentioned, this reason based on ecclesiology explains, on one hand, the "right" of lay associations to form, and on the other, the necessity of "criteria" for discerning the authenticity of the forms which such groups take in the Church.

First of all, the *freedom for lay people in the Church to form such groups* is to be acknowledged. Such liberty is a true and proper right that is not derived from any kind of "concession" by authority, but flows from the Sacrament of Baptism which calls the lay faithful to participate actively in the Church's communion and mission. In this regard the Council is quite clear: "As long as the proper relationship is kept to Church authority, the lay faithful have the right to found and run such associations and to join those already existing."[107] A citation from the recently published Code of Canon Law affirms it as well: "The Christian faithful are at liberty to found and govern associations for charitable and religious purposes or for the promotion of the Christian vocation in the world; they are free to hold meetings to pursue these purposes in common."[108]

It is a question of a freedom that is to be acknowledged and guaranteed by ecclesial authority and always and only to be exercised in Church communion. Consequently, the right of the lay faithful to form groups is essentially in relation to the Church's life of communion and to her mission.

"Criteria of Ecclesiality" for Lay Groups

30. It is always from the perspective of the Church's communion and mission, and not in opposition to the freedom to associate, that one understands the necessity of having *clear and definite criteria for discerning and recognizing* such lay groups, also called "Criteria of Ecclesiality."

The following basic criteria might be helpful in evaluating an association of the lay faithful in the Church:

—*The primacy given to the call of every Christian to holiness,* as it is manifested "in the fruits of grace which the spirit produces in the faithful"[109] and in a growth towards the fullness of Christian life and the perfection of charity.[110]

In this sense whatever association of the lay faithful there might be, it is always called to be more of an instrument leading to holiness in the Church, through fostering and promoting "a more intimate unity between the everyday life of its members and their faith."[111]

—The responsibility of professing the Catholic faith, embracing and proclaiming the truth about Christ, the Church and humanity, in obedience to the Church's Magisterium as the Church interprets it. For this reason every association of the lay faithful must be a *forum* where the faith is proclaimed as well as taught in its total content.

—The witness to a strong and authentic communion in filial relationship to the Pope, in total adherence to the belief that he is the perpetual and visible center of unity of the universal Church,[112] and with the local Bishop, "the visible principle and foundation of unity"[113] in the particular Church, and in "mutual esteem for all forms of the Church's apostolate."[114]

The communion with Pope and Bishop must be expressed in loyal readiness to embrace the doctrinal teachings and pastoral initiatives of both Pope and Bishop. Moreover, Church communion demands both an acknowledgment of a legitimate plurality of forms in the associations of the lay faithful in the Church and at the same time, a willingness to cooperate in working together.

—Conformity to and participation in the Church's apostolic goals, that is, "the evangelization and sanctification of humanity and the Christian formation of people's conscience, so as to enable them to infuse the spirit of the Gospel into the various communities and spheres of life."[115]

From this perspective, every one of the group forms of the lay faithful is asked to have a missionary zeal which will increase their effectiveness as participants in a re-evangelization.

—A commitment to a presence in human society which, in light of the Church's social doctrine, places it at the service of the total dignity of the person.

Therefore, associations of the lay faithful must become fruitful outlets for participation and solidarity in bringing about conditions that are more just and loving within society.

The fundamental criteria mentioned at this time find their verification in the *actual fruits* that various group forms show in their organizational life and the works they perform, such as: the renewed appreciation for prayer, contemplation, liturgical and sacramental life; the reawakening of vocations to Christian marriage, the ministerial priesthood and the consecrated life; a readiness to participate in programs and Church activities at the local, national and international levels; a commitment to catechesis and a capacity for teaching and forming Christians; a desire to be present as Christians in various settings of social life and the creation and awakening of charitable, cultural and spiritual works; the spirit of detachment and evangelical poverty leading to a greater generosity in charity towards all; conversion to the Christian life or the return to Church communion of those baptized members who have fallen away from the faith.

The Pastors in Service to Communion

31. The pastors of the Church, even if faced with possible and understandable difficulties as a result of such associations and the process of employing new forms, cannot renounce the service

provided by their authority, not simply for the well-being of the Church, but also for the well-being of the lay associations themselves. In this sense they ought to accompany their work of discernment with guidance and, above all, encouragement so that lay associations might grow in Church communion and mission.

It is exceedingly opportune that some new associations and movements receive *official recognition* and explicit approval from competent Church authority to facilitate their growth on both the national and international level. The Council has already spoken in this regard: "Depending on its various forms and goals, the lay apostolate provides for different types of relationships with the hierarchy.... Certain forms of the lay apostolate are given explicit recognition by the hierarchy, though in different ways. Because of the demands of the common good of the Church, moreover, ecclesial authority can select and promote in a particular way some of the apostolic associations and projects which have an immediately spiritual purpose, thereby assuming in them a special responsibility."[116]

Among the various forms of the lay apostolate which have a particular relationship to the hierarchy, the Synod Fathers have singled out various movements and associations of *Catholic Action* in which "indeed, in this organic and stable form, the lay faithful may freely associate under the movement of the Holy Spirit, in communion with their bishop and priests, so that in a way proper to their vocation and with some special method they might be of service through their faithfulness and good works to promote the growth of the entire Christian community, pastoral activities and infusing every aspect of life with the gospel spirit."[117]

The Pontifical Council for the Laity has the task of preparing a list of those associations which have received the official approval of the Holy See, and, at the same time, of drawing up, together with the Pontifical Council for the Union of Christians, the basic conditions on which this approval might be given to ecumenical associations in which there is a majority of Catholics, and determining those cases in which such an approval is not possible.[118]

All of us, pastors and lay faithful, have the duty to promote and nourish stronger bonds and mutual esteem, cordiality and collaboration among the various forms of lay associations. Only in this way can the richness of the gifts and charisms that the Lord offers us bear their fruitful contribution in building the common house: "For the sound building of a common house it is necessary, furthermore, that every spirit of antagonism and conflict be put aside and that the competition be in outdoing one another in showing honor (cf. Rom 12:10), in attaining a mutual affection, a will towards collaboration, with patience, farsightedness, and readiness to sacrifice which will at times be required."[119]

So as to render thanks to God for the great *gift* of Church communion which is the reflection in time of the eternal and ineffable communion of the love of God, Three in One, we once again consider Jesus' words: "I am the vine, you are the branches" (Jn 15:5). The awareness of the gift ought to be accompanied by a strong sense of *responsibility* for its use: it is, in fact, a gift that, like the talent of the gospel parable, must be put to work in a life of ever-increasing communion.

To be responsible for the gift of communion means, first of all, to be committed to overcoming each temptation to division and opposition that works against the Christian life with its responsibility in the apostolate. The cry of St. Paul continues to resound as a reproach to those who are "wounding the Body of Christ": "What I mean is that each one of you says, 'I belong to Paul,' or 'I belong to Cephas,' or 'I belong to Christ!' Is Christ divided?" (1 Cor 1:12-13) No, rather let these words of the Apostle sound a persuasive call: "I appeal to you, brethren, by the name of our Lord Jesus Christ, that all of you agree and that there be no dissensions among you, but that you be united in the same mind and the same judgment" (1 Cor 1:10).

Thus the life of Church communion will become a *sign* for all the world and a compelling *force* that will lead persons to faith in Christ: "that they may all be one; even as you, Father, are in me and I in you, that they also may be in us, so that the world may believe that you have sent me" (Jn 17:21). In such a way communion leads to *mission,* and mission itself to communion.

III

I Have Appointed You to Go Forth and Bear Fruit

The Co-responsibility of the Lay Faithful in the Church as Mission

Mission to Communion

32. We return to the biblical image of the vine and the branches which immediately and quite appropriately lends itself to a consideration of fruitfulness and life. Engrafted to the vine and brought to life, the branches are expected to bear fruit: "He who abides in me, and I in him, he it is that bears much fruit" (Jn 15:5). Bearing fruit is an essential demand of life in Christ and life in the Church. The person who does not bear fruit does not remain in communion: "Each branch of mine that bears no fruit, he [My Father] takes away" (Jn 15:2).

Communion with Jesus, which gives rise to the communion of Christians among themselves, is an indispensable condition for bearing fruit: "Apart from me you can do nothing" (Jn 15:5). And communion with others is the most magnificent fruit that the branches can give: in fact, it is the gift of Christ and his Spirit.

At this point *communion begets communion:* essentially it is likened to a *mission on behalf of communion.* In fact, Jesus says to his disciples: "You did not choose me, but I chose you and *appointed you that you should go and bear fruit* and that your fruit should abide" (Jn 15:16).

Communion and mission are profoundly connected with each other, they interpenetrate and mutually imply each other to the point that *communion represents both the source and the fruit of mission: communion gives rise to mission and mission is accomplished in communion.* It is always the one and the same Spirit who calls together and unifies the Church and sends her to preach the Gospel "to the ends of the earth" (Acts 1:8). On her part, the Church knows that the communion received by her as a gift is destined for all people. Thus the Church feels she owes to each individual and to humanity as a whole the gift received from the Holy Spirit that pours the charity of Jesus Christ into the hearts of believers, as a mystical force for internal cohesion and external growth. The mission of the Church flows from her own nature. Christ has willed it to be so: that of "sign and instrument...of unity of all the human race."[120] Such a mission has the purpose of making everyone know and live the "new" communion that the Son of God made man introduced into the history of the world. In this regard, then, the testimony of John the Evangelist defines in an undeniable way the blessed end towards which the entire mission of the Church is directed: "That which we have seen and heard we proclaim also to you, so that you may have fellowship with us; and our fellowship is with the Father and with his Son Jesus Christ" (1 Jn 1:3).

In the context of Church mission, then, *the Lord entrusts a great part of the responsibility to the lay faithful, in communion with all other members of the People of God.* This fact, fully understood by the Fathers of the Second Vatican Council, recurred with renewed clarity and increased vigor in all the works of the Synod: "Indeed, pastors know how much the lay faithful contribute to the welfare of the entire Church. They also know that they themselves were not established by Christ to undertake alone the entire saving mission of the Church towards the world, but they understand that it is their exalted office to be shepherds of the lay faithful and also to recognize the latter's services and charisms that all according to their proper roles may cooperate in this common undertaking with one heart."[121]

Proclaiming the Gospel

33. The lay faithful, precisely because they are members of the Church, have the vocation and mission of proclaiming the Gospel: they are prepared for this work by the sacraments of Christian initiation and by the gifts of the Holy Spirit.

In a very clear and significant passage from the Second Vatican Council we read: "As sharers in the mission of Christ, priest, prophet and king, the lay faithful have an active part to play in the life and activity of the Church.... Strengthened by their active participation in the liturgical life of their community, they are eager to do their share in apostolic works of that community. They lead to the Church people who are perhaps far removed from it; they earnestly cooperate in presenting the Word of God, especially by means of catechetical instruction; and offer their special skills to make the care of souls and the administration of the temporal goods of the Church more efficient."[122]

The entire mission of the Church, then, is concentrated and manifested in *evangelization*. Through the winding passages of history the Church has made her way under the grace and the command of Jesus Christ: "Go into all the world and preach the gospel to the whole creation" (Mk 16:15). "...and lo, I am with you always, until the close of the age" (Mt 28:20). "To evangelize," writes Paul VI, "is the grace and vocation proper to the Church, her most profound identity."[123]

Through evangelization the Church is built up into a *community of faith:* more precisely, into a community that *confesses* the faith in full adherence to the Word of God which is *celebrated* in the Sacraments and *lived* in charity, the principle of Christian moral existence. In fact, the "good news" is directed to stirring a person to a conversion of heart and life and a clinging to Jesus Christ as Lord and Savior; to disposing a person to receive Baptism and the Eucharist and to strengthen a person in the prospect and realization of new life according to the Spirit.

Certainly the command of Jesus: "Go and preach the Gospel" always maintains its vital value and its ever-pressing obligation. Nevertheless, the *present situation,* not only of the world but also of many parts of the Church, *absolutely demands that the word of Christ receive a more ready and generous obedience.* Every disciple is personally called by name; no disciple can withhold making a response: "Woe to me if I do not preach the gospel" (1 Cor 9:16).

The Hour Has Come for a Re-evangelization

34. Whole countries and nations where religion and the Christian life were formerly flourishing and capable of fostering a viable and working community of faith are now put to a hard test, and in some cases are even undergoing a radical transformation as a result of a constant spreading of an indifference to religion, of secularism and atheism. This particularly concerns countries and nations of the so-called First World in which economic well-being and consumerism, even if coexistent with a tragic situation of poverty and misery, inspires and sustains a life lived "as if God did not exist." This indifference to religion and the practice of religion devoid of true meaning in the face of life's very serious problems are not less worrying and upsetting when compared with declared atheism. Sometimes the Christian faith as well, while maintaining some of the externals of its tradition and rituals, tends to be separated from those moments of human existence which have the most significance, such as, birth, suffering and death. In such cases, the questions and formidable enigmas posed by these situations, if remaining without responses, expose contemporary people to an inconsolable delusion or to the temptation of

eliminating the truly humanizing dimension of life implicit in these problems.

On the other hand, in other regions or nations many vital traditions of piety and popular forms of Christian religion are still conserved; but today this moral and spiritual patrimony runs the risk of being dispersed under the impact of a multiplicity of processes, including secularization and the spread of sects. Only a re-evangelization can assure the growth of a clear and deep faith, and serve to make these traditions a force for authentic freedom.

Without doubt a mending of the Christian fabric of society is urgently needed in all parts of the world. But for this to come about what is needed is to *first remake the Christian fabric of the ecclesial community itself* present in these countries and nations.

At this moment the lay faithful, in virtue of their participation in the prophetic mission of Christ, are fully part of this work of the Church. Their responsibility, in particular, is to testify how the Christian faith constitutes the only fully valid response—consciously perceived and stated by all in varying degrees—to the problems and hopes that life poses to every person and society. This will be possible if the lay faithful will know how to overcome in themselves the separation of the Gospel from life, to again take up in their daily activities in family, work and society, an integrated approach to life that is fully brought about by the inspiration and strength of the Gospel.

To all people of today, I once again repeat the impassioned cry with which I began my pastoral ministry: *"Do not be afraid! Open, indeed, open wide the doors to Christ!* Open to his saving power the confines of states, and systems political and economic, as well as the vast fields of culture, civilization, and development. Do not be afraid! Christ knows 'what is inside a person.' Only he knows! Today too often people do not know what they carry inside, in the deepest recesses of their soul, in their heart. Too often people are uncertain about a sense of life on earth. Invaded by doubts they are led into despair. Therefore—with humility and trust I beg and implore you—allow Christ to speak to the person in you. Only he has the words of life, yes, eternal life." [124]

Opening wide the doors to Christ, accepting him into humanity itself poses absolutely no threat to persons, indeed it is the only road to take to arrive at the total truth and the exalted value of the human individual.

This vital synthesis will be achieved when the lay faithful know how to put the Gospel and their daily duties of life into a most shining and convincing testimony, where, not fear but the loving pursuit of Christ and adherence to him will be the factors determining how a person is to live and grow, and these will lead to new ways of living more in conformity with human dignity.

Humanity is loved by God! This very simple yet profound proclamation is owed to humanity by the Church. Each Christian's words and life must make this proclamation resound: God loves you, Christ came for you, Christ is for you "the Way, the Truth and the Life!" (Jn 14:6).

This re-evangelization is directed not only to individual persons but also to entire portions of populations in the variety of their situations, surroundings and cultures. Its purpose is the *formation of mature ecclesial communities* in which the faith might radiate and fulfill the basic meaning of adherence to the person of Christ and his Gospel, of an encounter and sacramental communion with him, and of an existence lived in charity and in service.

The lay faithful have their part to fulfill in the formation of these ecclesial communities, not only through an active and responsible participation in the life of the community, in other words, through a testimony that only they can give, but also through a missionary zeal and activity towards the many people who still do not believe and who no longer live the faith received at Baptism.

In the case of coming generations, the lay faithful must offer the very valuable contribution, more necessary than ever, of a *systematic work in catechesis*. The Synod Fathers have gratefully taken note of the work of catechists, acknowledging that they "have a task that carries great importance in animating ecclesial communities." [125] It goes without saying that Christian parents are the primary and irreplaceable catechists of their children, a task for which they are given the grace by the Sacrament of Matrimony. At the same time, however, we all ought to be aware of the "rights" that each baptized person has to being instructed, educated and supported in the faith and the Christian life.

Go into the Whole World

35. While pointing out and experiencing the present urgency for a re-evangelization, the Church cannot withdraw from *her ongoing mission of bringing the Gospel to the multitudes*—the millions and millions of men and women—*who as yet do not know Christ the Redeemer of humanity.* In a specific way this is the missionary work that Jesus entrusted and again entrusts each day to his Church.

The activity of the lay faithful, who are always present in these surroundings, is revealed in these days as increasingly necessary and valuable. As it stands, the command of the Lord "Go into the whole world" is continuing to find a generous response from laypersons who are ready to leave familiar surroundings, their work, their region or country, at least for a determined time, to go into mission territory. Even Christian married couples, in imitation of Aquila and Priscilla (cf. Acts 18; Rom 16:3ff.), are offering a comforting testimony of impassioned love for Christ and the Church through their valuable presence in mission lands. A true missionary presence is exercised even by those who for various reasons live in countries or surroundings where the Church is not yet established and bear witness to the faith.

However, at present the missionary concern is taking on such extensive and serious proportions for the Church that only a truly consolidated effort to assume responsibility by all members of the Church, both individuals and communities, can lead to the hope for a more fruitful response.

The invitation addressed by the Second Vatican Council to the particular Church retains all its value, even demanding at present a more extensive and more decisive acceptance: "Since the particular Churches are bound to mirror the universal Church as perfectly as possible, let them be fully aware that they have been sent also to those who do not believe in Christ." [126]

The Church today ought to take *a giant step forward* in her evangelization effort, and enter into *a new stage of history* in her missionary dynamism. In a world where the lessening of distance makes the world increasingly smaller, the Church community ought to strengthen the bonds among its members, exchange vital energies and means, and commit itself as a group to a unique and common mission of proclaiming and living the Gospel. "So-called younger Churches have need of the strength of the older Churches and the older ones need the witness and impulse of the younger, so that individual Churches receive the riches of other Churches." [127]

In this area, younger Churches are finding that an essential and undeniable element in the *founding of Churches*[128] is the formation not only of local clergy but also of a mature and responsible lay faithful: in this way the community which itself has been evangelized goes forth into a new region of the world so that it too might respond to the mission of proclaiming and bearing witness to the Gospel of Christ.

The Synod Fathers have mentioned that the lay faithful can favor the relations which ought to be established with followers of *various religions* through their example in the situations in which they live and in their activities: "Throughout the world today the Church lives among people of various religions.... All the Faithful, especially the lay faithful who live among the people of other religions, whether living in their native region or in lands as migrants, ought to be for all a sign of the Lord and his Church, in a way adapted to the actual living situation of each place. Dialogue among religions has a preeminent part for it leads to love and mutual respect, and takes away, or at least diminishes, prejudices among the followers of various religions and promotes unity and friendship among peoples." [129]

What is first needed for the evangelization of the world are *those who will evangelize.* In this regard everyone, beginning with the Christian family, must feel the responsibility to foster the birth and growth of *vocations*—both priestly and religious as well as in the lay state—*specifically directed to the missions.* This should be done by relying on every appropriate means, but without ever neglecting the privileged means of prayer, according to the very words of the Lord Jesus: "The harvest is plentiful, but the laborers are few; pray therefore the Lord of the harvest to send out laborers into his harvest!" (Mt 9:37, 38)

To Live the Gospel:
Serving the Person and Society

36. In both accepting and proclaiming the Gospel in the power of the Spirit, the Church becomes at one and the same time an "evangelizing and evangelized" community, and for this very

reason she is made the *servant of all*. In her the lay faithful participate in the mission of service to the person and society. Without doubt the Church has the Kingdom of God as her supreme goal, of which "she on earth is its seed and beginning," [130] and is therefore totally consecrated to the glorification of the Father. However, the Kingdom is the source of full liberation and total salvation for all people: with this in mind then, the Church walks and lives intimately bound in a real sense to their history.

Having received the responsibility of manifesting to the world the mystery of God that shines forth in Jesus Christ, *the Church likewise awakens one person to another,* giving a sense of one's existence, opening each to the whole truth about the individual and of each person's final destiny. [131] From this perspective the Church is called, in virtue of her very mission of evangelization, to serve all humanity. Such service is rooted primarily in the extraordinary and profound fact that "through the Incarnation the Son of God has united himself in some fashion to every person." [132]

For this reason the person "is the primary route that the Church must travel in fulfilling her mission: the individual is the *primary and fundamental way for the Church,* the way traced out by Christ himself, the way that leads invariably through the mystery of the Incarnation and Redemption." [133]

The Second Vatican Council, repeatedly and with a singular clarity and force, expressed these very sentiments in its documents. We again read a particularly enlightening text from the Constitution

Gaudium et Spes: "Pursuing the saving purpose which is proper to her, the Church not only communicates divine life to all, but in some way casts the reflected light of that divine life over the entire earth. She does this most of all by her healing and elevating impact on the dignity of the human person, by the way in which she strengthens the bonds of human society, and imbues the daily activity of people with a deeper sense and meaning. Thus, through her individual members and the whole community, the Church believes she can contribute much to make the family of man and its history more human." [134]

In this work of contributing to the human family, for which the whole Church is responsible, a particular place falls to the lay faithful, by reason of their "secular character," obliging them, in their proper and irreplaceable way, to work towards the Christian animation of the temporal order.

Promoting the Dignity of the Person

37. *To rediscover and make others rediscover the inviolable dignity of every human person* makes up an essential task, in a certain sense, the central and unifying task of the service which the Church and the lay faithful in her are called to render to the human family.

Among all other earthly beings, *only a man or a woman is a "person," a conscious and free being* and, precisely for this reason, the "center and summit" of all that exists on the earth. [135]

The dignity of the person is *the most precious*

possession of an individual. As a result, the value of one person transcends all the material world. The words of Jesus, "For what does it profit a man to gain the whole world and to forfeit his life?" (Mk 8:36) contain an enlightening and stirring statement about the individual: value comes not from what a person "has"—even if the person possessed the whole world!—as much as from what a person "is": the goods of the world do not count as much as the goods of the person, the good which is the person individually.

The dignity of the person is manifested in all its radiance when the person's origin and destiny are considered: created by God in his image and likeness as well as redeemed by the most precious blood of Christ, the person is called to be a "child in the Son" and a living temple of the Spirit, destined for the eternal life of blessed communion with God. For this reason every violation of the personal dignity of the human being cries out in vengeance to God and is an offense against the Creator of the individual.

In virtue of a personal dignity, the human being is *always a value as an individual,* and as such demands being considered and treated as a person and never, on the contrary, considered and treated as an object to be used or as a means or as a thing.

The dignity of the person constitutes *the foundation of the equality of all people among themselves.* As a result, all forms of discrimination are totally unacceptable especially those forms which unfortunately continue to divide and degrade the human family: from those based on race or economics to those social and cultural, from political to geographic, etc. Each discrimination constitutes an absolutely intolerable injustice, not so much for the tensions and the conflicts that can be generated in the social sphere, as much as for the dishonor inflicted on the dignity of the person: not only to the dignity of the individual who is the victim of the injustice, but still more to the one who commits the injustice.

Just as personal dignity is the foundation of equality of all people among themselves, so it is also *the foundation of participation and solidarity of all people among themselves:* dialogue and communion are rooted ultimately in what people "are," first and foremost, rather than on what people "have."

The dignity of the person is the indestructible property of *every human being.* The force of this affirmation is based on the *uniqueness and irrepeatability of every person.* From it flows that the individual can never be reduced by all that seeks to crush and to annihilate the person into the anonymity that comes from collectivity, institutions, structures and systems. As an individual, a person is not a number or simply a link in a chain, nor even less, an impersonal element in some system. The most radical and elevating affirmation of the value of every human being was made by the Son of God in his becoming man in the womb of a woman, as we continue to be reminded each Christmas.[136]

38. In effect, the acknowledgment of the personal dignity of every human being demands *the respect, the defense and the promotion of the rights of the human person.* It is a question of inherent, universal and inviolable rights. No one, no individual, no group, no authority, no state, can change—let alone eliminate—them because such rights find their source in God himself.

The inviolability of the person which is a reflection of the absolute inviolability of God, finds its primary and fundamental expression in the *inviolability of human life.* Above all, the common outcry, which is justly made on behalf of human rights—for example, the right to health, to home, to work, to family, to culture—is false and illusory if *the right to life,* the most basic and fundamental right and the condition for all other personal rights, is not defended with maximum determination.

The Church has never yielded in the face of all the violations that the right to life of every human being has received, and continues to receive, both from individuals and from those in authority. The human being is entitled to such rights *in every phase of development,* from conception until natural death; and *in every condition,* whether healthy or sick, whole or handicapped, rich or poor. The Second Vatican Council openly proclaimed: "All offenses against life itself, such as every kind of murder, genocide, abortion, euthanasia and willful suicide; all violations of the integrity of the human person, such as mutilation, physical and mental torture, undue psychological pressures; all offenses against human dignity, such as subhuman living conditions, arbitrary imprisonment, deportation, slavery, prostitution, the selling of women and children, degrading working conditions where men are treated as mere tools for profit rather than free and responsible persons; all these and the like are certainly criminal: they poison human society; and they do more harm to those who practice them than those who suffer from the injury. Moreover, they are a supreme dishonor to the Creator." [137]

If, indeed, everyone has the mission and responsibility of acknowledging the personal dignity of every human being and of defending the right to life, some lay faithful are given a particular title to this task: such as *parents, teachers, health care workers and the many who hold economic and political power.*

The Church today lives a fundamental aspect of her mission in lovingly and generously accepting every human being, especially those who are weak and sick. This is made all the more necessary as a "culture of death" threatens to take control. In fact, "the Church family believes that human life, even if weak and suffering, is always a wonderful gift of God's goodness. Against the pessimism and selfishness which casts a shadow over the world, the Church stands for life: in each human life she sees the splendor of that 'Yes,' that 'Amen,' which is Christ himself (cf. 2 Cor 1:19; Rev 3:14). To the 'No' which assails and afflicts the world, she replies with this living 'Yes,' this defending of the human person and the world from all who plot against life." [138] It is the responsibility of the lay faithful, who more directly through their vocation or their profession are involved in accepting life, to make the Church's "Yes" to human life concrete and efficacious.

The enormous development of *biological and medical science,* united to an amazing *power in technology,* today provides possibilities on the very frontier of human life which imply new responsibilities. In fact, today humanity is in the position not only of "observing" but even "exercising a control over" human life at its very beginning and in its first stages of development.

The *moral conscience* of humanity is not able to turn aside or remain indifferent in the face of these gigantic strides accomplished by a technology that is acquiring a continually more extensive and profound dominion over the working processes that govern procreation and the first phases of human life. Today as perhaps never before in history or in this field, *wisdom shows itself to be the only firm basis to salvation,* in that persons engaged in scientific research and in its application are always to act with intelligence and love, that is, respecting, even remaining in veneration of the inviolable dignity of the personhood of every human being from the first moment of life's existence. This occurs when science and technology are committed with licit means to the defense of life and the cure of disease in its beginnings, refusing on the contrary—even for the dignity of research itself—to perform operations that result in falsifying the genetic patrimony of the individual and of human generative power. [139]

The lay faithful, having responsibility in various capacities and at different levels of science as well as in the medical, social, legislative and economic fields must *courageously accept the "challenge" posed by new problems in bioethics*. The Synod Fathers used these words: "Christians ought to exercise their responsibilities as masters of science and technology, and not become their slaves.... In view of the moral challenges presented by enormous new technological power endangering not only fundamental human rights but the very biological essence of the human species, it is of utmost importance that lay Christians—with the help of the universal Church—take up the task of calling culture back to the principles of an authentic humanism, giving a dynamic and sure foundation to the promotion and defense of the rights of the human being in one's very essence—an essence which the preaching of the Gospel reveals to all.[140]

Today maximum vigilance must be exercised by everyone in the face of the phenomenon of the concentration of power and technology. In fact, such a concentration has a tendency to manipulate not only the biological essence but the very content of people's consciences and life-styles, thereby worsening the condition of entire peoples by discrimination and marginization.

Free to Call Upon
the Name of the Lord

39. Respect for the dignity of the person, which implies the defense and promotion of human rights, demands the recognition of the reli-

gious dimension of the individual. This is not simply a requirement "concerning matters of faith," but a requirement that finds itself inextricably bound up with the very reality of the individual. In fact, the individual's relation to God is a constitutive element of the very "being" and "existence" of an individual: it is in God that we "live, move and have our being" (Acts 17:28). Even if not all believe this truth, the many who are convinced of it have the right to be respected for their faith and for their life-choice, individual and communal, that flows from that faith. This is the *right of freedom of conscience and religious freedom,* the effective acknowledgment of which is among the highest goods and the most serious duties of every people that truly wishes to assure the good of the person and society. "Religious freedom, an essential requirement of the dignity of every person, is a cornerstone of the structure of human rights, and for this reason an irreplaceable factor in the good of individuals and of the whole of society, as well as of the personal fulfillment of each individual. It follows that the freedom of individuals and of communities to profess and practice their religion is an essential element for peaceful human coexistence.... The civil and social right to religious freedom, inasmuch as it touches the most intimate sphere of the spirit, is a point of reference for the other fundamental rights and in some way becomes a measure of them." [141]

The Synod did not forget the many brothers and sisters that still do not enjoy such a right and have to face difficulties, marginalization, suffering, persecution, and oftentimes death because of professing the faith. For the most part, they are brothers and sisters of the Christian lay faithful. The proclamation of the Gospel and the Christian testimony given in a life of suffering and martyrdom make up the summit of the apostolic life among Christ's disciples, just as the love for the Lord Jesus even to the giving of one's life constitutes a source of extraordinary fruitfulness for the building up of the Church. Thus the mystic vine bears witness to its earnestness in the faith, as expressed by St. Augustine: "But that vine, as predicted by the prophets and even by the Lord himself, spread its fruitful branches in the world, and becomes the more fruitful the more it is watered by the blood of martyrs." [142]

The whole Church is profoundly grateful for this example and this gift. These sons and daughters give reason for renewing the pursuit of a holy and apostolic life. In this sense the Fathers at the Synod have made it their special duty "to give thanks to those lay people who, despite their restricted liberty, live as tireless witnesses of faith in faithful union with the Apostolic See, although they may be deprived of sacred ministers. They risk everything, even life. In this way the lay faithful bear witness to an essential property of the Church: God's Church is born of God's grace which is expressed in an excellent way in martyrdom." [143]

Without doubt, all that has been said until now on the subject of respect for personal dignity and the acknowledgment of human rights concerns the responsibility of each Christian, of each person. However, we must immediately recognize how such a problem today has a *world dimension:* in fact, it is a question which at this moment affects entire groups, indeed entire peoples, who are violently being denied their basic rights. Those forms of unequal development among the so-called different "Worlds" were openly denounced in the recent Encyclical *Sollicitudo Rei Socialis.*

Respect for the human person goes beyond the demands of individual morality. Instead, it is a basic criterion, an essential element in the very structure of society, since the purpose of the whole of society itself is geared to the human person.

Thus, intimately connected with the responsibility of *service to the person* is the responsibility to *serve society,* as the general task of that Christian animation of the temporal order to which the lay faithful are called as their proper and specific role.

The Family:
Where the Duty to Society Begins

40. The human person has an inherent social dimension which calls a person from the innermost depths of self to *communion* with others and to the *giving* of self to others: "God, who has fatherly concern for everyone has willed that all people should form one family and treat one another in a spirit of brotherhood." [144] Thus, *society* as a fruit and sign of the *social nature* of the individual reveals its whole truth in being a *community of persons.*

Thus, the result is an interdependence and reciprocity between the person and society: all that is accomplished in favor of the person is also a service rendered to society, and all that is done in favor of society redounds to the benefit of the person. For this reason the duty of the lay faithful in the apostolate of the temporal order is always to be viewed both from its meaning of service to the person founded on the individual's uniqueness and irrepeatability as well as on the meaning of service to all people which is inseparable from it.

The first and basic expression of the social dimension of the person, then, is *the married couple and the family:* "But God did not create man a solitary being. From the beginning 'male and female he created them' (Gen 1:27). This partnership of man and woman constitutes the first form of communion between persons." [145] Jesus is concerned to restore integral dignity to the married couple and solidity to the family (Mt 19:3-9). St. Paul shows the deep rapport between marriage and the mystery of Christ and the Church (cf. Eph 5:22—6:4; Col 3:18-21; 1 Pt 3:1-7).

The *lay faithful's duty to society primarily begins* in marriage and in the family. This duty can only be fulfilled adequately with the conviction of the unique and irreplaceable value that the family has in the development of society and the Church herself.

The family is the basic cell of society. It is the cradle of life and love, the place in which the individual "is born" and "grows." Therefore a primary concern is reserved for this community, especially in those times when human egoism, the anti-birth campaign, totalitarian politics, situations of poverty, material, cultural and moral misery, threaten to make these very springs of life dry up.

Furthermore, ideologies and various systems, together with forms of uninterest and indifference, dare to take over the role in education proper to the family.

Required in the face of this is a vast, extensive and systematic work, sustained not only by culture but also by economic and legislative means, which will safeguard the role of family in its task of being the *primary place of "humanization"* for the person and society.

It is above all the lay faithful's duty in the apostolate to make the family aware of its identity as the primary social nucleus, and its basic role in society, so that it might itself become always a more *active and responsible place* for proper growth and proper participation in social life. In such a way the family can and must require from all, beginning with public authority, the respect for those rights which in saving the family will save society itself.

All that is written in the Exhortation *Familiaris Consortio* about participation in the development of society,[146] and all that the Holy See at the invitation of the 1980 Synod of Bishops has formulated with the "Charter of Rights for the Family," represent a complete and coordinated working program for all those members of the lay faithful who, in various capacities, are interested in the values and the needs of the family. Such a program needs to be more opportunely and decisively realized as the threats to the stability and fruitfulness of the family become more serious and the attempt to reduce the value of the family and to lessen its social value become more pressing and coordinated.

As experience testifies, whole civilizations and the cohesiveness of peoples depend above all on the human quality of their families. For this reason the duty in the apostolate towards the family acquires an incomparable social value. The Church, for her part, is deeply convinced of it, knowing well that "the path to the future passes through the family."[147]

Charity: The Soul and Sustenance of Solidarity

41. Service to society is expressed and realized in the most diverse ways, from those spontaneous and informal to those more structured; from help given to individuals to those destined for various groups and communities of persons.

The whole Church as such is directly called to the service of charity: "In the very early days the Church added the *agape* to the Eucharistic Supper, and thus showed herself to be wholly united around Christ by the bond of charity. So too, in all ages, she is recognized by this sign of love, and while she rejoices in the undertakings of others, she claims works of charity as her own inalienable duty and right. For this reason, mercy to the poor and the sick, works of charity and mutual aid intended to relieve human needs of every kind, are held in special honor in the Church."[148] *Charity towards one's neighbor,* through contemporary forms of the traditional spiritual and corporal works of mercy, represent the most immediate, ordinary and habitual ways that lead to the Christian animation of the temporal order, the specific duty of the lay faithful.

Through charity towards one's neighbor, the lay faithful exercise and manifest their participation in the kingship of Christ, that is, in the power of the Son of man who "came not to be served but to serve" (Mk 10:45). They live and manifest such a kingship in a most simple yet exalted manner, possible for everyone at all times because charity is the highest gift offered by the Spirit for building up the Church (cf. 1 Cor 13:13) and for the good of humanity. In fact, *charity gives life and sustains the works of solidarity that look to the total needs of the human being.*

The same charity, realized not only by individuals but also in a joint way by groups and communities, is and will always be necessary. Nothing and no one will be able to substitute for it, not even the multiplicity of institutions and public initiatives forced to give a response to the needs—oftentimes today so serious and widespread—of entire populations. Paradoxically such charity is made increasingly necessary the more that institutions become complex in their organization and pretend to manage every area at hand. In the end such projects lose their effectiveness as a result of an impersonal functionalism, an overgrown bureaucracy, unjust private interests and an all-too-easy and generalized disengagement from a sense of duty.

Precisely in this context various forms of *volunteer work* which express themselves in a multiplicity of services and activities continue to come about and to spread, particularly in organized society. If this impartial service be truly given for the good of all persons, especially the most in need and forgotten by the social services of society itself, then volunteer work can be considered an important expression of the apostolate in which lay men and women have a primary role.

Public Life:
for *Everyone and* by *Everyone*

42. A charity that loves and serves the person is never able to be separated from *justice.* Each in its own way demands the full, effective acknowledgment of the rights of the individual to which society is ordered in all its structures and institutions.[149]

In order to achieve their task directed to the Christian animation of the temporal order, in the sense of serving persons and society, the lay faithful *are never to relinquish their participation in "public life,"* that is, in the many different economic, social, legislative, administrative and cultural areas which are intended to promote organically and institutionally the *common good.* The Synod Fathers have repeatedly affirmed that every person has a right and duty to participate in public life, albeit in a diversity and complementarity of forms, levels, tasks and responsibilities. Charges of careerism, idolatry of power, egoism and corruption that are oftentimes directed at persons in government, parliaments, the ruling classes, or political parties, as well as the common opinion that participating in politics is an absolute moral danger, does not in the least justify either skepticism or an absence on the part of Christians in public life.

On the contrary, the Second Vatican Council's words are particularly significant: "The Church regards as worthy of praise and consideration the work of those who, as a service to others, dedicate themselves to the public good of the state and undertake the burdens of this task."[150]

Public life on behalf of the person and society finds its *basic standard* in *the pursuit of the common good,* as the good of *everyone* and as the good of each person taken as a *whole,* which is guaranteed and offered in a fitting manner to people both as individuals and in groups for their free and responsible acceptance. "The political community"—we read in the Constitution *Gaudium et Spes*—"exists for that common good in which the community finds its full justification and meaning, and from which it derives its basic, proper and lawful arrangement. The common good embraces the sum total of all those conditions of social life by which individuals, families and organizations can achieve more thoroughly their own fulfillment."[151]

Furthermore, public life on behalf of the person and society finds its *continuous line of action* in *the defense and the promotion of justice* understood to be a "virtue," an understanding which requires education, as well as a moral "force" that sustains the obligation to foster the rights and duties of each and everyone based on the personal dignity of each human being.

The spirit of service is a fundamental element in the exercise of political power. This spirit of service, together with the necessary competence and efficiency, can make "virtuous" or "above criticism" the activity of persons in public life which is justly demanded by the rest of the people. To accomplish this requires a full-scale battle and a determination to overcome every temptation, such as the recourse to disloyalty and to falsehood; the waste of public funds for the advantage of a few and those with special interests; and the use of ambiguous and illicit means for acquiring, maintaining and increasing power at any cost.

The lay faithful given a charge in public life certainly ought to respect the autonomy of earthly realities properly understood, as we read in the Constitution *Gaudium et Spes:* "It is of great importance, especially in a pluralistic society, to work out a proper vision of the relationship between the political community and the Church, and to distinguish clearly between the activities of Christians, acting individually or collectively in their own name as citizens guided by the dictates of a Christian conscience, and their activity in communion with their pastors in the name of the Church. The Church by reason of her role and competence is not identified with any political community nor bound by ties to any political system. She is at once the sign and the safeguard of the transcendental dimension of the human person."[152] At the same time—and this is felt today as a pressing responsibility—the lay faithful must bear witness to those human and gospel values that are intimately connected with political activity itself, such as liberty and justice, solidarity, faithful and unselfish dedication for the good of all, a simple life-style, and a preferential love for the poor and the least. This demands that the lay faithful always be more animated by a real participation in the life of the Church and enlightened by her social doctrine. In this they can be supported and helped by the nearness of the Christian community and their pastors.[153]

The manner and means for achieving a public life which has true human development as its goal is *solidarity*. This concerns the active and responsible *participation* of all in public life, from individual citizens to various groups, from labor unions to political parties. All of us, each and everyone, are the goal of public life as well as its leading participants. In this environment, as I wrote in the Encyclical *Sollicitudo Rei Socialis,* solidarity "is not a feeling of vague compassion or shallow distress at the misfortunes of so many people, both near and far. On the contrary, it is *a firm and persevering determination* to commit oneself to the *common good,* that is to say, to the good of all and of each individual because *we are all really responsible for all.*"[154]

Today political solidarity requires going beyond single nations or a single block of nations, to a consideration on a properly continental and world level.

The fruit of sound political activity, which is so much desired by everyone but always lacking in advancement, is *peace.* The lay faithful cannot remain indifferent or be strangers and inactive in the face of all that denies and compromises peace, namely: violence and war, torture and terrorism, concentration camps, militarization of public life, the arms race, and the nuclear threat. On the contrary, as disciples of Jesus Christ, "Prince of Peace" (Is 9:5) and "Our Peace" (Eph 2:14), the lay faithful ought to take upon themselves the task of being "peacemakers" (Mt 5:9), both through a conversion of "heart," justice and charity, all of which are the undeniable foundation of peace.[155]

The lay faithful in working together with all those that truly seek peace, and themselves serving in specific organizations as well as national and international institutions, ought to promote an extensive work of education intended to defeat the ruling culture of egoism, hate, the vendetta and hostility, and thereby to develop the culture of solidarity at every level. Such solidarity in fact "is *the way to peace and at the same time to development.*"[156] From this perspective the Synod Fathers have invited Christians to reject as unacceptable all forms of violence, to promote attitudes of dialogue and peace and to commit themselves to establish a just international and social order.[157]

Placing the Individual at the Center of Socio-Economic Life

43. Service to society on the part of the lay faithful finds its essence in the *socio-economic question* which depends on the organization of *work.*

Recently recalled in the Encyclical *Sollicitudo Rei Socialis,* is the seriousness of present problems as they relate to the subject of development and a proposed solution according to the social doctrine of the Church. I warmly desire to again refer its contents to all, in particular, to the lay faithful.

The basis for the social doctrine of the Church is the principle of *the universal destination of goods*. According to the plan of God the goods of the earth are offered to all people and to each individual as a means towards the development of a truly human life. At the service of this destination of goods is *private property,* which—precisely for this purpose—possesses an *intrinsic social function*. Concretely the *work* of man and woman represents the most common and most immediate instrument for the development of economic life, an instrument that constitutes at one and the same time a right and a duty for every individual.

Once again, all of this comes to mind in a particular way in the mission of the lay faithful. The Second Vatican Council formulates in general terms the purpose and criterion of their presence and their action: "In the socio-economic realm the dignity and total vocation of the human person must be honored and advanced along with the welfare of society as a whole, for man is the source, the center, and the purpose of all socio-economic life."[158]

In the context of the transformations taking place in the world of economy and work which are a cause of concern, the lay faithful have the responsibility of being in the forefront in working out a solution to the very serious problems of growing unemployment; to fight for the most opportune overcoming of numerous injustices that come from organizations of work which lack a proper goal; to make the workplace become a community of persons respected in their uniqueness and in their right to participation; to develop new solidarity among those that participate in a common work; to raise up new forms of business enterprising and to look again at systems of commerce, finance and exchange of technology.

To such an end the lay faithful must accomplish their work with professional competence, with human honesty, with a Christian spirit, and especially as a way of their own sanctification[159] according to the explicit invitation of the Council: "By work an individual ordinarily provides for self and family, is joined in fellowship to others, renders them service, and is enabled to exercise genuine charity and be a partner in the work of bringing divine creation to perfection. Moreover, we know that through work offered to God, an individual is associated with the redemptive work of Jesus Christ, whose labor with his hands at Nazareth greatly ennobled the dignity of work." [160]

Today in an ever-increasingly acute way, the *so-called "ecological" question* poses itself in relation to socio-economic life and work. Certainly humanity has received from God himself the task of "dominating" the created world and "cultivating the garden" of the world. But this is a task that humanity must carry out in respect for the divine image received, and therefore with intelligence and with love, assuming responsibility for the gifts that God has bestowed and continues to bestow. Humanity has in its possession a gift that must be passed on to future generations, if possible, passed on in better condition. Even these future generations are the recipients of the Lord's gifts: "The dominion granted to humanity by the Creator is not an absolute power, nor can one speak of a freedom to 'use and misuse,' or to dispose of things as one pleases. The limitation imposed from the beginning by the Creator himself and expressed symbolically by the prohibition not to 'eat of the fruit of the tree' (cf. Gen 2:16-17) shows clearly enough that, when it comes to the natural world we are subject not only to biological laws but also to moral ones which cannot be violated with impunity. A true concept of development cannot ignore the use of the things of nature, the renewability of resources and the consequences of haphazard industrialization—three considerations which alert our consciences to the *moral dimension* of development." [161]

Evangelizing Culture and the Cultures of Humanity

44. Service to the individual and to human society is expressed and finds its fulfillment through *the creation and the transmission of culture,* which especially in our time constitutes one of the more serious tasks of living together as a human family and of social evolution. In light of the Council, we mean by "culture" all those "factors which go to the refining and developing of humanity's diverse spiritual and physical endowments. It means the efforts of the human family to bring the world under its control through its knowledge and its labor; to humanize social life both in the family and in the whole civic community through the improvement of customs and insti-

tutions; to express through its works the great spiritual experiences and aspirations of all peoples throughout the ages; finally, to communicate and to preserve them to be an inspiration for the progress of many, indeed of the whole human race."[162] In this sense, culture must be held as the common good of every people, the expression of its dignity, liberty and creativity, and the testimony of its course through history. In particular, only from within and through culture does the Christian faith become a part of history and the creator of history.

The Church is fully aware of a pastoral urgency that calls for an absolutely special concern for culture in those circumstances where the development of a culture becomes disassociated not only from Christian faith but even from human values,[163] as well as in those situations where science and technology are powerless in giving an adequate response to the pressing questions of truth and well-being that burn in people's hearts. For this reason the Church calls upon the lay faithful to be present as signs of courage and intellectual creativity in the privileged places of culture, that is, the world of education—school and university—in places of scientific and technological research, the areas of artistic creativity and work in the humanities. Such a presence is destined not only for the recognition and possible purification of the elements that critically burden existing culture, but also for the elevation of these cultures through the riches which have their source in the Gospel and the Christian faith. The extensive treatment by the Second Vatican Council of the rapport between the Gospel and culture represents a constant historic fact and at the same time serves as a working ideal of particular and immediate urgency. It is a challenging program given as a pastoral responsibility to the entire Church, but in a specific way to her faithful. "The good news of Christ continually renews the life and culture of fallen humanity; it combats and removes the error and evil which flow from the attraction of sin which are a perpetual threat. She never ceases to purify and to elevate the morality of peoples.... In this way the Church carries out her mission and in that very act she stimulates and makes her contribution to human and civic culture. By her action, even in its liturgical forms, she leads people to interior freedom." [164]

Some particularly significant citations from Paul VI's Exhortation *Evangelii Nuntiandi* merit recollection here: "The Church evangelizes when she seeks to convert, solely through the divine power of the message she proclaims (cf. Rom 1:16; 1 Cor 1:18; 2:4), both the personal and collective consciences of people, the activities in which they engage, and the lives and concrete milieux which are theirs. Strata of humanity are transformed: for the Church it is a question not only of preaching the Gospel in ever-wider geographic areas or to ever-greater numbers of people, but also of affecting and as it were challenging through the power of the Gospel, mankind's criteria of judgment, determining values, points of interest, lines of thought, sources of inspiration and models of life, which are in contrast with the Word of God and the plan of salvation. All this could be expressed in the following words: What matters is to evangelize humanity's culture and the cultures of the human family.... The split between the Gospel and culture is without a doubt the drama of our time, just as it was of other times. Therefore, every effort must be made to ensure a full evangelization of culture, or more correctly of cultures." [165]

The privileged way at present for the creation and transmission of culture is the *means of social communications*. [166] The world of the mass media represents a new frontier for the mission of the Church because it is undergoing a rapid and innovative development and has an extensive worldwide influence on the formation of mentality and customs. In particular, the lay faithful's responsibility as professionals in this field, exercised both by individual right and through community initiatives and institutions, demands a recognition of all its values, and demands that it be sustained by more adequate resource materials, both intellectual and pastoral.

The use of these instruments by professionals in communication, and their reception by the public demand both a work of education in a critical sense which is animated by a passion for the truth, and a work of defense of liberty, respect for the dignity of individuals, and the elevation of the authentic culture of peoples which occurs through a firm and courageous rejection of every form of monopoly and manipulation.

However, the pastoral responsibility among

the lay faithful does not stop with this work of defense. It extends to everyone in the world of communications, even to those professional people of the press, cinema, radio, television and theater. These also are called to proclaim the Gospel that brings salvation.

IV
Laborers in the Lord's Vineyard

Good Stewards of God's Varied Grace

The Variety of Vocations

45. According to the gospel parable, the "householder" calls the laborers for his vineyard at *various* times during the day: some at dawn, others about nine in the morning, still others about midday and at three, the last, around five (cf. Mt 20:1ff.). In commenting on these words of the Gospel, St. Gregory the Great makes a comparison between the various times of the call and the different *stages in life:* "It is possible to compare the different hours," he writes, "to the various stages in a person's life. According to our analogy the morning can certainly represent childhood. The third hour then, can refer to adolescence; the sun has now moved to the height of heaven, that is, at this stage a persons grows in strength. The sixth hour is adulthood, the sun is in the middle of the sky, indeed at this age the fullness of vitality is obvious. Old age represents the ninth hour because the sun starts its descent from the height of heaven, thus the youthful vitality begins to decline. The eleventh hour represents those who are most

advanced in years.... The laborers, then, are called and sent forth into the vineyard at different hours, that is to say, one is led to a holy life during childhood, another in adolescence, another in adulthood and another in old age."[167]

We can make a further application of the comments of St. Gregory the Great to the extraordinary variety of ways the Church becomes "present" in life; one and all are called to work for the coming of the Kingdom of God according to the diversity of callings and situations, charisms and ministries. This variety is not only linked to age, but also to the difference of sex and to the diversity of natural gifts as well as to careers and conditions affecting a person's life. It is a variety that makes the riches of the Church more vital and concrete.

Young People, Children and Older People

Youth, the Hope of the Church

46. The Synod wished to *give particular attention to the young.* And rightly so. In a great many countries of the world, they represent half of entire populations, and often constitute in number half of the People of God itself living in those countries. Simply from this aspect youth make up an exceptional potential and a *great challenge for the future of the Church.* In fact, the Church sees her path towards the future in the youth— beholding in them a reflection of herself and her call to that blessed youthfulness which she constantly enjoys as a result of Christ's Spirit. In this

sense the Council has defined youth as "the hope of the Church." [168]

In the letter of March 31, 1985 to young men and women in the world we read: "The Church looks to the youth, indeed the Church in a special way *looks at herself in the youth,* in all of you and in each of you. It has been so from the beginning, from apostolic times. The words of St. John in his *First Letter* can serve as special testimony: 'I am writing to you, *young people,* because *you have overcome the evil one.* I write to you, children, because *you know the Father....* I write to you, *young people,* because *you are strong* and the word of God *abides in you* (1 Jn 2:13ff.).... In our generation, at the end of the Second Millennium after Christ, the Church also sees herself in the youth." [169]

Youth must not simply be considered as an object of pastoral concern for the Church: in fact, young people are and ought to be encouraged to be active on behalf of the Church as *leading characters in evangelization and participants in the renewal of society.* [170] Youth is a time of an especially intensive *discovery* of a "self" and a "choice of life." It is a time for *growth* which ought to progress "in wisdom, age and grace before God and people" (Lk 2:52).

The Synod Fathers have commented: "The sensitivity of young people profoundly affects their perceiving of the values of justice, non-violence and peace. Their hearts are disposed to fellowship, friendship and solidarity. They are greatly moved by causes that relate to the quality of life and the conservation of nature. But they are troubled by anxiety, deceptions, anguishes and fears of the world as well as by the temptations that come with their state." [171]

The Church must seek to rekindle the very special love displayed by Christ towards the young man in the Gospel: "Jesus, looking upon him, loved him" (Mk 10:21). For this reason the Church does not tire of proclaiming Jesus Christ, of proclaiming his Gospel as the unique and satisfying response to the most deep-seated aspirations of young people as illustrated in Christ's forceful and exalted personal call to discipleship ("Come and follow me." Mk 10:21) that brings about a sharing in the filial love of Jesus for his Father and the participation in his mission for the salvation of humanity.

The Church has so much to talk about with youth, and youth have so much to share with the Church. This mutual dialogue, by taking place with great cordiality, clarity and courage, will provide a favorable setting for the meeting and exchange between generations, and will be a source of richness and youthfulness for the Church and civil society. In its message to young people the Council said: "The Church looks to you with confidence and with love.... She is the real youthfulness of the world.... Look upon the Church and you will find in her the face of Christ." [172]

Children and the Kingdom of Heaven

47. Children are certainly the object of the Lord Jesus' tender and generous love. To them he gave his blessing, and even more, to them he promised the Kingdom of heaven (cf. Mt 19:13-

15; Mk 10:14). In particular Jesus exalted the active role that little ones have in the Kingdom of God. They are the eloquent symbol and exalted image of those moral and spiritual conditions that are essential for entering into the Kingdom of God and for living the logic of total confidence in the Lord: "Truly I say to you, unless you turn and become like children, you will never enter the Kingdom of heaven. Whoever humbles himself like this child, he is the greatest in the Kingdom of heaven" (Mt 18:3-5; cf. Lk 9:48).

Children are a continual reminder that the missionary fruitfulness of the Church has its life-giving basis not in human means and merits, but in the absolute gratuitous gift of God. The life itself of innocence and grace of many children, and even the suffering and oppression unjustly inflicted upon them are in virtue of the Cross of Christ a source of spiritual enrichment for them and for the entire Church. Everyone ought to be more conscious and grateful for this fact.

Furthermore, it must be acknowledged that valuable possibilities exist even in the life's stages of infancy and childhood, both for the building up of the Church and for making society more humane. How often the Council referred to the beneficial and constructive affects for the family, "the domestic Church," through the presence of sons and daughters: "Children as living members of the family, contribute in their own way to the sanctification of their parents." [173] The Council's words must also be repeated about children in relation to the local and universal Church. John Gerson, a great theologian and educator of the 15th Century, had already emphasized this fact in stating that "children and young people are in no way a negligible part of the Church." [174]

Older People and the Gift of Wisdom

48. I now address older people, oftentimes unjustly considered as unproductive if not directly an insupportable burden. I remind older people that the Church calls and expects them to continue to exercise their mission in the apostolic and missionary life. This is not only a possibility for them, but it is their duty even in this time in their life when age itself provides opportunities in some specific and basic way.

The Bible delights in presenting the older person as the symbol of someone rich in wisdom and fear of the Lord (cf. Sir 25:4-6). In this sense the "gift" of older people can be specifically that of being the witness to tradition in the faith, both in the Church and in society (cf. Ps 44:2; Ex 12:26-27), the teacher of the lessons of life (cf. Sir 6:34; 8:11-12), and the worker of charity.

At this moment the growing number of older people in different countries worldwide and the expected retirement of persons from various professions and the workplace provides older people with a new opportunity in the apostolate. Involved in the task is their determination to overcome the temptation of taking refuge in a nostalgia—in a never-to-return past—or fleeing from present responsibility because of difficulties encountered in a world of one novelty after another. They must always have a clear knowledge that one's role in the Church and society does not stop at a certain age at all, but at such times knows only new ways of application. As the Psalmist says: "They still bring forth fruit in old age, they are ever full of sap and green, to show that the Lord is upright" (Ps 92:15-16). I repeat all that I said during the celebration of the Older People's Jubilee: "Arriving at an older age is to be considered a privilege: not simply because not everyone has the good fortune to reach this stage in life, but also, and above all, because this period provides real possibilities for better evaluating the past, for knowing and living more deeply the Paschal Mystery, for becoming an example in the Church for the whole People of God.... Despite the complex nature of the problems you face: a strength that progressively diminishes, the insufficiencies of social organizations, official legislation that comes late, or the lack of understanding by a self-centered society, you are not to feel yourselves as persons underestimated in the life of the Church or as passive objects in a fast-paced world, but as participants at a time of life which is humanly and spiritually fruitful. You still have a mission to fulfill, a contribution to make. According to the divine plan, each individual human being lives a life of continual growth, from the beginning of existence to the moment at which the last breath is taken." [175]

Women and Men

49. The Synod Fathers gave special attention to the status and role of women, with two purposes in mind: to themselves acknowledge and to invite all others to once again acknowledge the indispen-

sable contribution of women to the building up of the Church and the development of society. They wished as well to work on a more specific analysis of women's participation in the life and mission of the Church.

Making reference to Pope John XXIII, who saw women's greater consciousness of their proper dignity and their entrance into public life as signs of our times,[176] the Synod Fathers, when confronted with the various forms of discrimination and marginalization to which women are subjected simply because they are women, time and time again strongly affirmed the urgency to defend and to promote the *personal dignity of women,* and consequently her equality with man.

If anyone has this task of advancing the dignity of women in the Church and society, it is women themselves who must recognize their responsibility as leading characters. There is still much effort to be done in many parts of the world and in various surroundings to destroy that unjust and deleterious mentality which considers the human being as a thing, as an object to buy and sell, as an instrument for selfish interests or for pleasure only. Women themselves, for the most part, are the prime victims of such a mentality. Only through openly acknowledging the personal dignity of women is the first step taken to promote the full participation of women in Church life as well as in social and public life. A more extensive and decisive response must be given to the demands made in the Exhortation *Familiaris Consortio* concerning the many discriminations of which women are the victims: "Vigorous and incisive pastoral action must be taken by all to overcome completely these forms of discrimination so that the image of God that shines in all human beings without exception may be fully respected." [177] Along the same lines, the Synod Fathers stated: "As an expression of her mission, the Church must stand firmly against all forms of discrimination and abuse of women." [178] And again: "The dignity of women, gravely wounded in public esteem, must be restored through effective respect for the rights of the human person and by putting the teaching of the Church into practice." [179]

In particular when speaking of *active and responsible participation in the life and mission of the Church,* emphasis should be placed on what has already been stated and clearly urged by the Second Vatican Council: "Since in our days women are taking an increasingly active share in the whole life of society, it is very important that they participate more widely also in the various fields of the Church's apostolate." [180]

The awareness that women with their own gifts and tasks have *their own specific vocation,* has increased and been deepened in the years following the Council and has found its fundamental inspiration in the Gospel and the Church's history. In fact, for the believer, the Gospel— namely, the word and example of Jesus Christ— remains the necessary and decisive point of reference. In no other moment in history is this fact more fruitful and innovative.

Though not called to the apostolate of the Twelve, and thereby to the ministerial priesthood, many women nevertheless accompanied Jesus in his ministry and assisted the group of Apostles (cf. Lk 8:2-3); were present at the foot of the Cross (cf. Lk 23:49); assisted at the burial of Christ (cf. Lk 23:55); received and transmitted the message of resurrection on Easter morn (cf. Lk 24:1-10); and prayed with the Apostles in the Cenacle awaiting Pentecost (cf. Acts 1:14).

From the evidence of the Gospel, the Church at its origin detached herself from the culture of the time and called women to tasks connected with spreading the Gospel. In his letters the Apostle Paul even cites by name a great number of women for their various functions in service of the primitive Christian community (cf. Rom 16:1-15; Phil 4:2-3; Col 4:15 and 1 Cor 11:5; 1 Tim 5:16). "If the witness of the Apostles founds the Church," stated Paul VI, "the witness of women contributes greatly towards nourishing the faith of Christian communities." [181]

Both in her earliest days and in her successive development, the Church, albeit in different ways and with diverse emphases, has always known women who have exercised an oftentimes decisive role in the Church herself and accomplished tasks of considerable value on her behalf. History is marked by grand works, quite often lowly and hidden, but not for this reason any less decisive to the growth and the holiness of the Church. It is necessary that this history continue, indeed that it be expanded and intensified in the face of the growing and widespread awareness of the personal dignity of woman and her vocation, particularly in light of the urgency of a "re-evangelization" and a major effort towards "humanizing" social relations.

Gathering together the pronouncements of the Second Vatican Council which reflect the Gospel's message and the Church's history, the Synod Fathers formulated, among others, this precise "recommendation": "It is necessary that the Church recognize all the gifts of men and women for her life and mission, and put them into practice." [182] And again, "This Synod proclaims that the Church seeks the recognition and use of all the gifts, experiences and talents of men and women to make her mission effective (cf. Congregation for the Doctrine of the Faith, *Instruction on Christian Freedom and Liberation*, 72)." [183]

Anthropological and Theological Foundations

50. The condition that will assure the rightful presence of woman in the Church and in society is a more penetrating and accurate consideration of the *anthropological foundation for masculinity and femininity* with the intent of clarifying woman's personal identity in relation to man, that is, a diversity yet mutual complementarity, not only as it concerns roles to be held and functions to be performed, but also, and more deeply, as it concerns her make-up and meaning as a person. The Synod Fathers have deeply felt this requirement, maintaining that "the anthropological and theological foundations for resolving questions about the true significance and dignity of each sex require deeper study." [184]

Through committing herself to a reflection on the anthropological and theological basis of femininity, the Church enters the historic process of the various movements for the promotion of woman, and in going to the very basic aspect of woman as a personal being, provides her most precious contribution. But even before this the Church intends, in such a way, to obey God who created the individual "in his image," "male and female he created them" (Gen 1:27) and who intended that they would accept the call of God to come to know, reverence and live his plan. It is a plan that "from the beginning" has been indelibly imprinted in the very being of the human person—men and women—and therefore in the make-up, meaning and deepest workings of the individual. This most wise and loving plan must be explored to discover all its richness of content—a richness that "from the beginning" came to be progressively manifested and realized in the whole history of salvation, and was brought to completion in "the fullness of time," when "God sent his Son, born of a woman" (Gal 4:4). That "fullness" continues in history: God's plan for woman is read and is to be read within the context of the faith of the Church, and also in the lives lived by so many Christian women today. Without forgetting the help that can come from different human sciences and cultures, researchers, because of an informed discernment, will be able to help gather and clarify the values and requirements that belong to the enduring essential aspects of women and those bound to evolve in history. The Second Vatican Council reminds us: "The Church maintains that beneath all changes there are many realities which do not change; these find their ultimate foundation in Christ who is the same yesterday, and today, and forever (cf. Heb 13:8)." [185] The Apostolic Letter on the Dignity and Vocation of Woman gives much attention to the anthropological and theological foundation of woman's dignity as a person. The document seeks to again treat and develop the catechetical reflections of the Wednesday General Audiences devoted over a long period of time to the "theology of the body," while at the same time fulfilling a promise made in the Encyclical *Redemptoris Mater*[186] and serving as a response to the request of the Synod Fathers.

May the reading of the Apostolic Letter *Mulieris Dignitatem* in particular, as a biblical-theological meditation, be an incentive for everyone—women and men—and especially for those who devote their lives to the human sciences and theological disciplines, to pursue on the basis of the personal dignity of man and woman and their mutual relationship, a critical study to better and more deeply understand the values and specific gifts of femininity and masculinity—not only in the surroundings of social living but also and above all in living as Christians and as members of the Church.

This meditation on the anthropological and theological foundations of women ought to enlighten and guide the Christian response to the most frequently asked questions, oftentimes so crucial, on *the "place" that women can have and ought to have in the Church and in society.*

It is quite clear from the words and attitude of Christ, which are normative for the Church, that no discrimination exists on the level of an individual's relation to Christ, in which "there is neither male nor female; for you are all one in Christ Jesus" (Gal 3:28) and on the level of participation in the Church's life of grace and holiness, as Joel's prophecy fulfilled at Pentecost wonderfully attests: "I will pour out my spirit on all flesh; your sons and daughters shall prophecy" (Joel 3:1; cf. Acts 2:17ff.). As the Apostolic Letter on the Dignity and Vocation of Woman reads: "Both women and men...are equally capable of receiving the outpouring of divine truth and love in the Holy Spirit. Both receive his salvific and sanctifying 'visits.'" [187]

Mission in the Church and in the World

51. In speaking about participation in the apostolic mission of the Church, there is no doubt that in virtue of Baptism and Confirmation, a woman—as well as a man—is made a sharer in the threefold mission of Jesus Christ, Priest, Prophet and King, and is thereby charged and given the ability to fulfill the fundamental apostolate of the Church: *evangelization.* However, a woman is called to put to work in this apostolate the "gifts" which are properly hers: first of all, the gift that is her very dignity as a person exercised in word and testimony of life, gifts therefore connected with her vocation as a woman.

In her participation in the life and mission of the Church, a woman cannot receive the *Sacrament of Orders,* and therefore cannot fulfill the proper function of the ministerial priesthood. This is a practice that the Church has always found in the expressed will of Christ, totally free and sovereign, who called only men to be his apostles;[188] a practice that can be understood from the rapport between Christ, the Spouse, and his Bride, the Church.[189] Here we are in the area of *function,* not of *dignity* and *holiness.* In fact, it must be maintained: "Although the Church possesses a 'hierarchical' structure, nevertheless this structure is totally ordered to the holiness of Christ's members."[190]

However, as Paul VI has already said, "We cannot change what our Lord did, nor his call to women; but we can recognize and promote the role of women in the mission of evangelization and in the life of the Christian community."[191]

Above all, the *acknowledgment in theory* of the active and responsible presence of woman in the Church must be *realized in practice.* With this in mind this Exhortation addressed to the lay faithful with its deliberate and repeated use of the terms "women and men," must be read. Furthermore the revised Code of Canon Law contains many provisions on the participation of women in the life and mission of the Church: they are provisions that must be more commonly known and, according to the diverse sensibilities of culture and opportuneness in a pastoral situation, be realized with greater timeliness and determination.

An example comes to mind in the participation of women on diocesan and parochial Pastoral Councils as well as Diocesan Synods and particular councils. In this regard the Synod Fathers have written: "Without discrimination women should be participants in the life of the Church and also in consultation and the process of coming to decisions." [192] And again: "Women, who already hold places of great importance in transmitting the faith and offering every kind of service in the life of the Church, ought to be associated in the preparation of pastoral and missionary documents and ought to be recognized as cooperators in the mission of the church in the family, in professional life and in the civil community." [193]

In the more specific area of evangelization and catechesis, the particular work that women have in the transmission of the faith, not only in the family but also in the various educational environments, is to be more strongly fostered. In broader terms, this should be applied in all that regards embracing the Word of God, its understanding and its communication as well as its study, research and theological teaching.

While she is to fulfill her duty to evangelize, woman is to feel more acutely her need to be evangelized. Thus, with her vision illumined by faith (cf. Eph 1:18), woman is to be able to distinguish what truly responds to her dignity as a person and to her vocation from all that, under the pretext of this "dignity" and in the name of "freedom" and "progress," militates against true values. On the contrary, these false values become responsible for the moral degradation of the person, the environment and society. This same "discernment," made possible and demanded from Christian women's participation in the prophetic mission of Christ and his Church, recurs with continued urgency throughout history. This "discernment," often mentioned by the Apostle Paul, is not only a matter of evaluating reality and events in the light of faith, but also involves a real decision and obligation to employ it, not only in Church life but also in human society.

It can be said that the problems of today's world already cited in the second part of the Council's Constitution *Gaudium et Spes,* which remain unresolved and not at all affected by the passage of time, must witness the presence and commitment of women with their irreplaceable and customary contributions.

In particular, two great tasks entrusted to women merit the attention of everyone.

First of all, the task of *bringing full dignity to the conjugal life and to motherhood.* Today new possibilities are opened to women for a deeper understanding and a richer realization of human and Christian values implied in the conjugal life and the experience of motherhood. Man himself—husband and father—can be helped to overcome forms of absenteeism and of periodic presence as well as a partial fulfillment of parental responsibilities—indeed he can be involved in new and significant relations of interpersonal communion—precisely as a result of the intelligent, loving and decisive intervention of woman.

Secondly, women have the task of *assuring the moral dimension of culture,* the dimension—namely of *a culture worthy of the person*—of an individual yet social life. The Second Vatican Council seems to connect the moral dimension of culture with the participation of the lay faithful in the kingly mission of Christ: "Let the lay faithful by their combined efforts remedy the institutions and conditions of the world when the latter are an inducement to sin, that all such things may be conformed to the norms of justice, and may favor the practice of virtue rather than hindering it. By so doing, they will infuse culture and human works with a moral value."[194]

As women increasingly participate more fully and responsibly in the activities of institutions which are associated with safeguarding the basic duty to human values in various communities, the words of the Council just quoted point to an important field in the apostolate of women: in all aspects of the life of such communities, from the socio-economic to the socio-political dimension, the personal dignity of woman and her specific vocation ought to be respected and promoted. Likewise this should be the case in living situations not only affecting the individual but also communities, not only in forms left to personal freedom and responsibility, but even in those guaranteed by just civil laws.

"It is not good for man to be alone: let us make him a helper fit for him" (Gen 2:18). *God entrusted the human being to woman.* Certainly, every human being is entrusted to each and every other human being, but in a special way the human being is entrusted to woman, precisely because the woman in virtue of her special experience of motherhood is seen to have a *specific sensitivity* towards the human person and all that constitutes the individual's true welfare, beginning with the fundamental value of life. How great are the possibilities and responsibilities of woman in this area at a time when the development of science and technology is not always inspired and measured by true wisdom, with the inevitable risk of "de-humanizing" human life, above all when it would demand a more intense love and a more generous acceptance.

The participation of women in the life of the Church and society in the sharing of her gifts is likewise the path necessary for her personal fulfillment—on which so many justly insist today—and the basic contribution of woman to the enrichment of Church communion and the dynamism in the apostolate of the People of God.

From this perspective the presence also of men, together with women, ought to be considered.

The Presence and Collaboration of Men Together with Women

52. Many voices were raised in the Synod Hall expressing the fear that excessive insistence given to the status and role of women would lead to an unacceptable omission, that in point, regarding *men*. In reality, various sectors in the Church must lament the absence or the scarcity of the presence of men, some of whom abdicate their proper Church responsibilities, allowing them to be fulfilled only by women. Such instances are participation in the liturgical prayer of the Church, education and, in particular, catechesis of their own sons and daughters and other children; presence at religious and cultural meetings; and collaboration in charitable and missionary initiatives.

Therefore, the coordinated presence of both men and women is to be pastorally urged so that the participation of the lay faithful in the salvific mission of the Church might be rendered more rich, complete and harmonious.

The fundamental reason that requires and explains the presence and the collaboration of both men and women is not only, as it was just emphasized, the major source of meaning and efficacy in the pastoral action of the Church, nor even less is it the simple sociological fact of sharing a life together as human beings which is natural for man and woman. It is, rather, the original plan of the Creator who from the "beginning" willed the human being to be a "unity of the two," and willed man and woman to be the prime community of persons, source of every other community, and at the same time to be a "sign" of that interpersonal communion of love which constitutes the mystical, intimate life of God, One in Three.

Precisely for this reason, the most common and widespread way, and at the same time, fundamental way to assure this coordinated and harmonious presence of men and women in the life and mission of the Church, is the fulfillment of the tasks and responsibilities of the couple and the Christian family in which the variety of diverse forms of life and love is seen and communicated: conjugal, paternal and maternal, filial and familial. We read in the Exhortation *Familiaris Consortio:* "Since the Christian family is a community in which the relationships are renewed by Christ through faith and the sacraments, the family's sharing in the Church's mission should follow *a community pattern:* the spouses together *as a couple,* the parents and children *as a family,* must live their service to the Church and to the world.... The Christian family also builds up the Kingdom of God in history through the everyday realities that concern and distinguish its *state of life:* it is thus in the *love between husband and wife and between members of the family*—a love lived out in all its extraordinary richness of values and demands: totality, oneness, fidelity and fruitfulness—that the Christian family's participation in the prophetic, priestly and kingly mission of Jesus Christ and of his Church finds expression and realization." [195]

From this perspective, the Synod Fathers have recalled the meaning that the Sacrament of Matrimony ought to assume in the Church and society in order to illuminate and inspire all the relations between men and women. In this regard they have emphasized an "urgent need for every Christian to live and proclaim the message of hope contained in the relation between man and woman. The Sacrament of Matrimony, which consecrates this relation in its conjugal form and reveals it as a sign of the relation of Christ with his Church, contains a teaching of great importance for the Church's life—a teaching that ought to reach today's world through the Church; all those relations between man and woman must be imbued by this spirit. The Church should even more fully rely on the riches found here." [196] These same Fathers have rightly emphasized that "the esteem for virginity and reverence for motherhood must be respectively restored," [197] and still again they have called for the development of diverse and complementary vocations in the living context of Church communion and in the service of its continued growth.

The Sick and the Suffering

53. People are called to joy. Nevertheless, each day they experience many forms of suffering and pain. The Synod Fathers in addressing men and women affected by these various forms of suffering and pain used the following words in their final *Message:* "You who are the abandoned and pushed to the edges of our consumer society; you who are sick, people with disabilities, the poor and hungry, migrants and prisoners, refugees, unemployed, abandoned children and old people who feel alone; you who are victims of war and all kinds of violence—the Church reminds you that she shares your suffering. She takes it to the Lord who in turn associates you with his redeeming Passion. You are brought to life in the light of his resurrection. We need you to teach the whole world what love is. We will do everything we can so that you may find your rightful place in the Church and in society." [198]

In the context of such a limitless world as human suffering, we now turn our attention to all those struck down by sickness in its various forms: sickness is indeed the most frequent and common expression of human suffering.

The Lord addresses his call to each and every one. *Even the sick are sent forth as laborers into the Lord's vineyard:* the weight that wearies the body's members and dissipates the soul's serenity is far from dispensing a person from working in the vineyard. Instead the sick are called to live their human and Christian vocation and to participate in the growth of the Kingdom of God in a *new and even more valuable manner.* The words of the Apostle Paul ought to become their approach to life, or better yet cast an illumination to permit them to see the meaning of grace in their very situation: "In my flesh I complete what is lacking in Christ's afflictions for the sake of his body, that is, the Church" (Col 1:24). Precisely in arriving at this realization, the Apostle is raised up in joy: "I rejoice in my sufferings for your sake" (Col 1:24). In the same way many of the sick can become bearers of the "joy inspired by the Holy Spirit in much affliction" (1 Thes 1:6) and witnesses to Jesus' resurrection. A handicapped person expressed these sentiments in a presentation in the Synod Hall: "It is very important to make clear that Christians who live in situations of illness, pain and old age are called by God not only to unite their suffering to Christ's Passion but also to receive in themselves now, and to transmit to others, the power of renewal and the joy of the risen Christ (cf. 2 Cor 4:10-11; 1 Pt 4:13; Rom 8:18ff.)." [199]

On the Church's part—as it reads in the Apostolic Letter *Salvifici Doloris*—"Born in the mystery of Redemption in the Cross of Christ, the Church has to try to *meet* man in a special way on the path of suffering. In this meeting, man 'becomes the way for the Church,' and this is one of the most important ways." [200] At this moment *the suffering individual is the way of the Church* because that person is, first of all, the way of Christ himself who is the Good Samaritan who "does not pass by," but "has compassion on him, went to him...bound up his wounds...took care of him" (Lk 10:32-34).

From century to century the Christian community in revealing and communicating its healing love and the consolation of Jesus Christ, has reenacted the gospel parable of the Good Samaritan in caring for the vast multitude of persons who are sick and suffering. This came about through the untiring commitment of all those who have taken care of the sick and suffering as a result of science and the medical arts, as well as the skilled and generous service of health care workers. Today there is an increase in the presence of lay women and men in Catholic hospital and health care institutions. At times the lay faithful's presence in these institutions is total and exclusive. It is to just such people—doctors, nurses, other health care workers, volunteers—that the call becomes the living sign of Jesus Christ and his Church in showing love towards the sick and suffering.

Renewed Pastoral Action

54. It is necessary that this most precious heritage which the Church has received from Jesus Christ, "Physician of the body and the spirit,"[201] must never diminish but must always come to be more valued and enriched through renewal and decisive initiatives of *pastoral activity for and with the sick and suffering*. This activity must be capable of sustaining and fostering attention, nearness, presence, listening, dialogue, sharing and real help towards individuals in moments when sickness and suffering sorely test not only faith in life but also faith in God and his love as Father.

One of the basic objectives of this renewed and intensified pastoral action, which must involve all components of the ecclesial community in a coordinated way, is an attitude which looks upon the sick person, the bearer of a handicap, or the suffering individual, not simply as an *object* of the Church's love and service, but as an *active and responsible participant in the work of evangelization and salvation.* From this perspective the Church has to let the good news resound within a society and culture which, having lost the sense of human suffering, "censors" all talk on such a hard reality of life. The good news is the proclamation that suffering can even have a positive meaning for the individual and for society itself, since each person is called to a form of participation in the salvific suffering of Christ and in the joy of resurrection, as well as, thereby, to become a force for the sanctification and building up of the Church.

The proclamation of this good news gains credibility when it is not simply voiced in words, but passes into a testimony of life, both in the case of all those who lovingly care for the sick, the handicapped and the suffering, as well as the suffering themselves who are increasingly made more conscious and responsible of their place and task within and on behalf of the Church.

In order that "the civilization of love" can flourish and produce fruit in this vast world of human pain, I invite all to reread and meditate on the Apostolic Letter *Salvifici Doloris* from which I am pleased to again propose the lines from its conclusion: "There should come together in spirit beneath the Cross of Calvary all suffering people who believe in Christ, and particularly those who suffer because of their faith in him who is the Crucified and Risen One, so that the offering of their sufferings may hasten the fulfillment of the prayer of the Savior himself, that all may be one. Let there also gather beneath the Cross all people of good will, for on this Cross is the 'Redeemer of Man,' the Man of Sorrows, who has taken upon himself the physical and moral sufferings of the people of all times, so that *in love* they may find the salvific meaning of their sorrow and valid answers to all their questions.

"Together with Mary, Mother of Christ who *stood beneath the Cross,* we pause beside all the crosses of contemporary man and we ask all of you *who suffer* to support us. We ask precisely you who are weak to *become a source of strength* for the Church and humanity. In the terrible battle between the forces of good and evil revealed to our eyes by our modern world, may your sufferings in union with the Cross of Christ be victorious." [202]

The States of Life and Vocations

55. All the members of the People of God—clergy, men and women religious, the lay faithful—are laborers in the vineyard. At one and the same time they are all the goal and subjects of Church communion as well as of participation in the mission of salvation. Every one of us possessing charisms and ministries, diverse yet complementary, works in the one and the same vineyard of the Lord.

Simply in *being* Christians, even before actually *doing* the works of a Christian, all are branches of the one fruitful vine which is Christ. All are living members of the one Body of the Lord built up through the power of the Spirit. The significance of "being" a Christian does not come about simply from the life of grace and holiness which is the primary and more productive source of the apostolic and missionary fruitfulness of Holy Mother Church. Its meaning also arises from the state of life that characterizes the clergy, men and women religious, members of secular institutes and the lay faithful.

In Church Communion the states of life, by being ordered one to the other, are thus bound together among themselves. They all share in a deeply basic meaning: that of being *the manner of living out the commonly shared Christian dignity and the universal call to holiness in the perfection of love.* They are *different yet complementary* in the sense that each of them has a basic and unmistakable character which sets each apart, while at the same time each of them is seen in relation to the other and placed at each other's service.

Thus the *lay* state of life has its distinctive feature in its secular character. It fulfills an ecclesial service in bearing witness and, in its own way recalling for priests, women and men religious, the significance of the earthly and temporal realities in the salvific plan of God. In turn, the *ministerial* priesthood represents in different times and places, the permanent guarantee of the sacramental presence of Christ the Redeemer. The religious state bears witness to the eschatalogical character of the Church, that is, the straining towards the Kingdom of God that is prefigured and in some

143

way anticipated and experienced even now through the vows of chastity, poverty and obedience.

All the states of life, whether taken collectively or individually in relation to the others, are at the service of the Church's growth. While different in expression they are deeply united in the Church's "mystery of communion" and are dynamically coordinated in its unique mission.

Thus in the diversity of the states of life and the variety of vocations this same, unique mystery of the Church reveals and experiences anew *the infinite richness of the mystery of Jesus Christ.* The Fathers were fond of referring to the Church as a field of a pleasing and wonderful variety of herbs, plants, flowers and fruits. St. Ambrose writes: "A field produces many fruits, but the one which has an abundance of both fruits and flowers is far better. The field of holy Church is fruitful in both one and the other. In this field there are the priceless buds of virginity blossoming forth, widowhood stands out boldly as the forest in the plain; elsewhere the rich harvest of weddings blessed by the Church fills the great granary of the world with abundant produce, and the wine-presses of the Lord Jesus overflow with the grapes of a productive vine, enriching Christian marriages." [203]

The Various Vocations in the Lay State

56. The Church's rich variety is manifested still further from within each state of life. Thus *within the lay state diverse "vocations" are given,* that is, there are different paths in the spiritual life and the apostolate which are taken by individual members of the lay faithful. In the field of a

"commonly shared" lay vocation, "special" lay vocations flourish. In this area we can also recall the spiritual experience of the flourishing of diverse forms of secular institutes that have developed recently in the Church. These offer the lay faithful, and even priests, the possibility of professing the evangelical counsels of poverty, chastity and obedience through vows or promises, while fully maintaining one's lay or clerical state.[204] In this regard the Synod Fathers have commented, "The Holy Spirit stirs up other forms of self-giving to which people who remain fully in the lay state devote themselves."[205]

We can conclude by reading a beautiful passage taken from St. Francis de Sales, who promoted lay spirituality so well.[206] In speaking of "devotion," that is Christian perfection or "life according to the Spirit," he presents in a simple yet insightful way the vocation of all Christians to holiness while emphasizing the specific form with which individual Christians fulfill it: "In creation God commanded the plants to bring forth their fruits, each one after its kind. So does he command all Christians who are the living plants of his Church, to bring forth the fruits of devotion, each according to his character and vocation. Devotion must be exercised in different ways by the gentleman, the workman, the servant, the prince, the widow, the maiden and the married woman. Not only this, but the practice of devotion must also be adapted to the strength, the employment, and the duties of each one in particular.... It is an error, or rather a heresy, to try to banish the devout life from the regiment of soldiers, the shop of the mechanic, the court of princes, or the home of married folk. It is true, Philothea, that a purely contemplative, monastic and religious devotion cannot be exercised in such ways of life. But besides these three kinds of devotion, there are several others adapted to bring to perfection those who live in the secular state." [207]

Along the same line the Second Vatican Council states: "This lay spirituality should take its particular character from the circumstances of one's state in life (married and family life, celibacy, widowhood), from one's state of health and from one's professional and social activity. All should not cease to develop earnestly the qualities and talents bestowed on them in accord with these conditions of life and should make use of the gifts which they have received from the Holy Spirit." [208]

What has been said about the spiritual vocation can also be said—and to a certain degree with greater reason—of the infinite number of ways through which all members of the Church are employed as laborers in the vineyard of the Lord, building up the Mystical Body of Christ. Indeed, as a person with a truly unique life story, each is called by name to make a special contribution to the coming of the Kingdom of God. No talent, no matter how small, is to be hidden or left unused (cf. Mt 25:24-27).

In this regard the Apostle Peter gives us a stern warning: "As each has received a gift, employ it for one another, as good stewards of God's varied grace" (1 Pt 4:10).

V

That You Bear Much Fruit

The Formation of the Lay Faithful

A Continual Process of Maturation

57. The gospel image of the vine and the branches reveals to us another fundamental aspect of the lay faithful's life and mission: *the call to growth and a continual process of maturation, of always bearing much fruit.*

As a diligent vinedresser, the Father takes care of his vine. God's solicitude is so ardently called upon by Israel that she prays: "Turn again, O God of hosts! / Look down from heaven, and see; / have regard for this vine, / the stock which your right hand has planted" (Ps 80:15-16). Jesus himself speaks of the Father's work: "I am the true vine, and my Father is the vinedresser. Every branch of mine that bears no fruit he takes away, and every branch that does bear fruit he prunes, that it may bear more fruit" (Jn 15:1-2).

The vitality of the branches depends on their remaining attached to the vine which is Jesus Christ: *"He who abides in me and I in him bears much fruit,* for apart from me you can do nothing" (Jn 15:5).

People are approached in liberty by God who calls everyone to grow, develop and bear fruit. A person cannot put off a response nor cast off personal responsibility in the matter. The solemn words of Jesus refer to this exalted and serious responsibility: "If a man does not abide in me, he is cast forth as a branch and withers; and the branches are gathered, thrown into the fire and burned" (Jn 15:6).

In this dialogue between God who offers his gifts, and the person who is called to exercise responsibility, there comes the possibility, indeed the necessity, of a total and ongoing formation of the lay faithful, as the Synod Fathers have rightly emphasized in much of their work. After having described Christian formation as "a continual process in the individual of maturation in faith, and a likening to Christ according to the will of the Father, under the guidance of the Holy Spirit," they have clearly affirmed that the formation of the lay faithful must be placed *among the priorities of a diocese.* "It ought to be so placed within the *plan of pastoral action* that the efforts of the whole community (clergy, lay faithful and religious) converge on this goal." [209]

To Discover and Live One's Vocation and Mission

58. The fundamental objective of the formation of the lay faithful is an ever-clearer discovery of one's vocation and the ever-greater willingness to live it so as to fulfill one's mission.

God calls me and sends me forth as a laborer in his vineyard. He calls me and sends me forth work for the coming of his Kingdom in history. This personal vocation and mission defines the dignity and the responsibility of each member of the lay faithful and makes up the focal point of the whole work of formation, whose purpose is the joyous and grateful recognition of this dignity and the faithful and generous living-out of this responsibility.

In fact, from eternity God has thought of us and has loved us as unique individuals. Every one of us he called by name, as the Good Shepherd "calls his sheep by name" (Jn 10:3). However, only in the unfolding of the history of our lives and its events is the eternal plan of God revealed to each of us. Therefore, it is a gradual process; in a certain sense, one that happens day by day.

To be able to discover the actual will of the Lord in our lives always involves the following: a receptive listening to the Word of God and the Church, fervent and constant prayer, recourse to a wise and loving spiritual guide, and a faithful discernment of the gifts and talents given by God, as well as the diverse social and historic situations in which one lives.

Therefore, in the life of each member of the lay faithful there are *particularly significant and decisive moments* for discerning God's call and embracing the mission entrusted by him. Among these are the periods of *adolescence* and *young adulthood*. No one must forget that the Lord, as the master of the laborers in the vineyard, calls *at every hour* of life so as to make his holy will more precisely and explicitly known. Therefore, the fundamental and continuous attitude of the disciple

should be one of vigilance and a conscious atten-
tiveness to the voice of God.

It is not a question of simply *knowing* what
God wants from each of us in the various situations of life. The individual must *do* what God
wants, as we are reminded in the words that Mary,
the Mother of Jesus, addressed to the servants at
Cana: "Do whatever he tells you" (Jn 2:5). However, to act in fidelity to God's will requires a
capability for acting and *the developing of that
capability.* We can rest assured that this is possible
through the free and responsible collaboration of
each of us with the grace of the Lord which is
never lacking. St. Leo the Great says: "The one
who confers the dignity will give the strength!" [210]

This then is the marvelous yet demanding task
awaiting all the lay faithful and all Christians at
every moment: to grow always in the knowledge of
the richness of Baptism and faith as well as to live
it more fully. In referring to birth and growth as
two stages in the Christian life, the Apostle Peter
makes the following exhortation: "Like newborn
babes, long for the pure spiritual milk, that by it
you may grow up to salvation" (1 Pt 2:2).

A Total Integrated Formation
for Living an Integrated Life

59. In discovering and living their proper vocation and mission, the lay faithful must be formed
according to the *union* which exists from their
being *members of the Church and citizens of human society.*

There cannot be two parallel lives in their
existence: on the one hand, the so-called "spiri-

tual" life, with its values and demands; and on the other, the so-called "secular" life, that is, life in a family, at work, in social relationships, in the responsibilities of public life and in culture. The branch, engrafted to the vine which is Christ, bears its fruit in every sphere of existence and activity. In fact, every area of the lay faithful's lives, as different as they are, enters into the plan of God who desires that these very areas be the "places in time" where the love of Christ is revealed and realized for both the glory of the Father and service of others. Every activity, every situation, every precise responsibility—as, for example, skill and solidarity in work, love and dedication in the family and the education of children, service to society and public life and the promotion of truth in the area of culture—are the occasions ordained by Providence for a "continuous exercise of faith, hope and charity." [211]

The Second Vatican Council has invited all the lay faithful to this *unity of life* by forcefully decrying the grave consequences in separating faith from life, and the Gospel from culture: "The Council exhorts Christians, as citizens of one city and the other, to strive to perform their earthly duties faithfully in response to the spirit of the Gospel. They are mistaken who, knowing that we have here no abiding city but seek one which is to come, think that they may therefore shirk their earthly responsibilities; for they are forgetting that by faith itself they are more than ever obliged to measure up to these duties, each according to one's vocation.... This split between the faith which many profess and their daily lives deserves to be counted among the more serious errors of our age." [212] Therefore, I have maintained that a faith that does not affect a person's culture is a faith "not fully embraced, not entirely thought out, not faithfully lived." [213]

Various Aspects of Formation

60. The many interrelated aspects of a *totally integrated formation* of the lay faithful are situated within this unity of life.

There is no doubt that *spiritual* formation ought to occupy a privileged place in a person's life. Everyone is called to grow continually in intimate union with Jesus Christ, in conformity to the Father's will, in devotion to others in charity and justice. The Council writes: "This life of intimate union with Christ in the Church is nourished by spiritual helps available to all the faithful, especially by active participation in the liturgy. Lay people should so make use of these helps in such a way that, while properly fulfilling their secular duties in the ordinary conditions of life, they do not disassociate union with Christ from that life, but through the very performance of their tasks according to God's will, may they actually grow in it." [214]

The situation today points to an ever-increasing urgency for *a doctrinal* formation of the lay faithful, not simply in a better understanding which is natural to faith's dynamism but also in enabling them to "give a reason for their hoping" in view of the world and its grave and complex problems. Therefore, a systematic approach to *catechesis,* geared to age and the diverse situations of life, is an absolute necessity, as is a more decided Christian promotion of *culture,* in response to the perennial yet always new questions that concern individuals and society today.

This is especially true for the lay faithful who have responsibilities in various fields of society and public life. Above all, it is indispensable that they have a more exact knowledge—and this demands a more widespread and precise presentation—of the *Church's social doctrine* as repeatedly stressed by the Synod Fathers in their presentations. They refer to the participation of the lay faithful in public life in the following words: "But for the lay faithful to take up actively this noble purpose in political matters, it is not enough to exhort them. They must be offered a proper formation of a social conscience, especially in the Church's social teaching, which contains principles of reflection, criteria for judging and practical directives (cf. Congregation for the Doctrine of the Faith, *Instruction on Christian Freedom and Liberation,* 72), and which must be present in general catechetical instruction and in specialized gatherings, as well as in schools and universities. Nevertheless, this social doctrine of the Church is dynamic; that is, adapted to circumstances of time and place. It is the right and duty of pastors to propose moral principles even concerning the social order, and of all Christians to apply them in defense of human rights.... Nevertheless, active participation in political parties is reserved to the lay faithful." [215]

The cultivation of *human values* finds a place in the context of a totally integrated formation, bearing a particular significance for the missionary and apostolic activities of the lay faithful. In this regard the Council wrote: "[the lay faithful] should also hold in high esteem professional skill, family and civic spirit, and the virtues related to social behavior, namely, honesty, a spirit of justice, sincerity, courtesy, moral courage; without them there is no true Christian life." [216]

In bringing their lives into an organic synthesis, which is at one and the same time, the manifestation of the unity of "who they are" in the Church and society as well as the condition for the effective fulfillment of their mission, the lay faithful are to be guided interiorly and sustained by the Holy Spirit who is the Spirit of unity and fullness of life.

Collaborators with God the Teacher

61. Where are the lay faithful formed? What are the means of their formation? Who are the *persons and the communities* called upon to assume the task of a totally integrated formation of the lay faithful?

Just as the work of human education is intimately connected with fatherhood and motherhood, so Christian formation finds its origin and its strength in God the Father who loves and educates his children. Yes, *God is the first and great teacher of his People,* as it states in the striking passage of the Song of Moses: "He found him in a desert land / and in the howling waste of the wilderness; / he encircled him, he cared for him, he kept him as the apple of his eye. / Like an eagle that stirs up its nest, that flutters over its young, spreading out its wings, catching them, bearing them on its pinions, / the Lord alone did lead him, and there was no foreign God with him" (Deut 32:10-12; cf. 8:5).

God's work in forming his people is revealed and fulfilled in Jesus Christ the Teacher, and reaches to the depths of every individual's heart as a result of the living presence of the Spirit. *Mother Church* is called to take part in the divine work of formation, both through a sharing of her very life, and through her various pronouncements and actions. It is thus that the *lay faithful are formed by the Church and in the Church* in a mutual communion and collaboration of all her members: clergy, religious and lay faithful. Thus the whole ecclesial community, in its diverse members, receives the fruitfulness of the Spirit and actively cooperates towards that end. With this in mind Methodius of Olympo wrote: "Those not yet perfected are carried and formed by those more perfect, as in the womb of a mother, until the time they are generated and brought forth for the greatness and beauty of virtue." [217] This happened with St. Paul who was carried and brought forth in the Church by those who were perfected (in the person of Ananias), and then Paul in his turn became perfected and fruitful in bringing forth many children.

First of all, the Church is a teacher in which the Pope takes the "primary" role in the formation of the lay faithful. As successor of St. Peter he has the ministry of "confirming his brothers in the faith," instructing all believers in the essential content of vocation and mission in light of the Christian faith and membership in the Church. Therefore, not simply the words coming directly from him, but also those transmitted by the various departments of the Holy See call for a living and receptive hearing by the lay faithful.

The one and universal Church is present in various parts of the world, in and through the *particular Churches*. In each of them the Bishop in his person has a responsibility towards the lay faithful in forming the animation and guidance of their Christian life through the proclamation of the Word and the celebration of the Eucharist and the Sacraments.

Situated and at work within the particular Church or diocese is the *Parish* which has the essential task of a more personal and immediate formation of the lay faithful. In fact, because it is in the position to reach more easily individual persons and singular groups, the parish is called to instruct its members in hearing God's Word, in liturgical and personal dialogue with God, in the life of fraternal charity, and in allowing a more direct and concrete perception of the sense of ecclesial communion and responsibility in the Church's mission.

Internal to the parish, especially if vast and territorially extensive, *small Church communities,* where present, can be a notable help in the formation of Christians by providing a consciousness and an experience of ecclesial communion and mission which are more extensive and incisive. The Synod Fathers have said that a post-baptismal catechesis in the form of a catechumenate can also be helpful by presenting again some elements from the Rite of Christian Initiation of Adults with the purpose of allowing a person to grasp and live the immense, extraordinary richness and responsibility received at Baptism.[218]

In the formation that the lay faithful receive from their diocese and parish, especially concerning communion and mission, the help that diverse members of the Church can give to each other is particularly important. This mutual help also aids in revealing the mystery of the Church as Mother and Teacher. Priests and religious ought to assist the lay faithful in their formation. In this regard the Synod Fathers have invited priests and candidates for Orders to "be prepared carefully so that they are ready to foster the vocation and mission of the lay faithful."[219] In turn, the lay faithful themselves can and should help priests and religious in the course of their spiritual and pastoral journey.

Other Places for Formation

62. The *Christian family,* as the "domestic Church," also makes up a natural and fundamental school for formation in the faith: father and mother receive from the Sacrament of Matrimony the grace and the ministry of the Christian education of their children before whom they bear witness and to whom they transmit both human and religious values. While learning their first words, children learn also the praise of God whom they feel is near them as a loving and providential Father; while learning the first acts of love, children also learn to open themselves to others, and through the gift of self receive the sense of living

as a human being. The daily life itself of a truly Christian family makes up the first "experience of Church," intended to find confirmation and development in an active and responsible process of the children's introduction into the wider ecclesial community and civil society. The more that Christian spouses and parents grow in the awareness that their "domestic church" participates in the life and mission of the universal Church, so much the more will their sons and daughters be able to be formed in a "sense of the Church" and will perceive all the beauty of dedicating their energies to the service of the Kingdom of God.

Schools and Catholic universities, as well as centers of spiritual renewal which are becoming ever more widespread in these days, are also important places for formation. In the present social and historical context which is marked by an extensively deep cultural involvement, the Synod Fathers have emphasized that parents' participation in school life—besides being always necessary and without substitution—is no longer enough. What is needed is to prepare the lay faithful to dedicate themselves to the work of rearing their children as a true and proper part of Church mission. What is needed is to constitute and develop this "formation community" which is together comprised of parents, teachers, clergy, women and men religious and representatives of youth. In order that the school can suitably fulfill its natural function in formation, the lay faithful ought to feel charged to demand from everyone and for everyone a true freedom in education, even through opportune civil legislation.[220]

The Synod Fathers expressed words of esteem and encouragement to all those lay faithful, both women and men, who with a civic and Christian spirit, fulfill a task which is involved in the education of children both in schools and institutes of formation. In addition they have emphasized the urgent need in various schools, whether Catholic or not, for teachers and professors among the lay faithful to be true witnesses of the Gospel through their example of life, their professional competence and uprightness, their Christian inspired teaching, preserving always—as is obvious—the autonomy of various sciences and disciplines. It is of singular importance that scientific and technological research done by the faithful be correct from the standpoint of service to an individual in the totality of the context of one's values and needs: to these lay faithful the Church entrusts the task of allowing all to better understand the intimate bond that exists between faith and science, between the Gospel and human culture.[221]

"This Synod"—we read in the proposition—"appeals to the prophetic task of Catholic schools and universities, and praises teachers and professors, now lay people for the most part, for their dedication to maintaining institutes of Catholic education that can form men and women in whom the new commandment is enfleshed. The simultaneous presence of clergy, the lay faithful and men and women religious, offers students a vivid image of the Church and makes recognition of its riches easier" (cf. Congregation for Catholic Education, *Concerning the Lay Educator, Witness of Faith in the Schools*).[222]

Groups, associations and movements also have their place in the formation of the lay faithful. In fact, they have the possibility, each with its own method, of offering a formation through a deeply shared experience in the apostolic life, as well as having the opportunity to integrate, to make concrete and specific the formation that their members receive from other persons and communities.

The Reciprocal Formation
Received and Given by All

63. Formation is not the privilege of a few, but a right and duty of all. In this regard the Synod Fathers have said: "Possibilities of formation should be proposed to all, especially the poor, who can also be a source of formation for all"; and they added: "Suitable means to help each person fulfill a full, human and Christian vocation should be applied to formation." [223]

For the purpose of a truly incisive and effective pastoral activity, the *formation of those who will form others* is to be developed through appropriate courses or suitable schools. Forming those who in turn will be given the responsibility for the formation of the lay faithful, constitutes a basic requirement of assuring the general and widespread formation of all the lay faithful.

According to the explicit invitation of the Synod Fathers, special attention ought to be devoted to the local culture in the work of formation: "The formation of Christians will take the greatest account of local human culture which contributes to formation itself, and will help to discern the value, whether implanted in tradition or proposed in modern affairs. Attention should be paid to diverse cultures which can exist in one and the same people or nation at the same time. The Church, the mother and teacher of peoples, should strive to safeguard, where the need exists, the culture of a less numerous people living in large nations when the situation exists." [224]

In the work of formation some convictions reveal themselves as particularly necessary and fruitful. First of all, there is the conviction that one cannot offer a true and effective formation to others if the individual has not taken on or developed a personal responsibility for formation: this, in fact, is essentially a "formation of self."

In addition, there is the conviction that at one and the same time each of us is the goal and principle of formation: the more we are formed and the more we feel the need to pursue and deepen our formation, still more will we be formed and be rendered capable of forming others.

It is particularly important to know that the work of formation, while having intelligent recourse to the means and methods available from human science, is made more effective the more it is open to the *action of God*. Only the branch which does not fear being pruned by the heavenly vinedresser can bear much fruit for the individual and for others.

An Appeal and a Prayer

64. At the conclusion of this post-synodal document I once again put forward the invitation of "the householder" proposed in the Gospel: *You too go into my vineyard.* It can be said that the significance of the Synod on the vocation and mission of the lay faithful might very well consist in this *call of the Lord which he addresses to everyone,* yet in a particular way to the lay faithful, both women and men.

The happenings at the Synod have been a great spiritual experience for all the participants. The experience has been that of a Church under the light and the power of the Spirit, intent on discerning and embracing the renewed call of her Lord so that she can again propose to today's world the mystery of her communion and the dynamism of her mission of salvation, especially by centering on the specific place and role of the lay faithful. This Exhortation then, intends to urge the most abundant possible fruitfulness from this Synod in every part of the Church worldwide. This will come about as a result of an effective hearkening to the Lord's call by the entire People of God, in particular by the lay faithful.

Therefore I make a strong appeal to one and all, pastors and faithful, never to become tired of maintaining—indeed always taking an active part to fix deeply in one's mind, heart and life—an *ecclesial consciousness* which is ever mindful of what it means to be members of the Church of Jesus Christ, participants in her mystery of communion and in her dynamism in mission and the apostolate.

It is of particular importance that all Christians be aware that through Baptism they have received an *extraordinary dignity:* through grace we are called to be children loved by the Father, members incorporated in Christ and his Church, living and holy temples of the Spirit. With deep emotion and gratitude, we again hear the words of John the Evangelist: "See what love the Father has given us, that we should be called children of God; and so we are" (1 Jn 3:1).

While this "Christian *newness of life"* given to the members of the Church constitutes for all the basis of their participation in the priestly, prophetic and kingly mission of Christ and of their vocation to holiness in love, it receives expression and is fulfilled in the lay faithful through the "secular character" which is "uniquely and properly" theirs.

Besides imparting an awareness of a commonly shared Christian dignity, an ecclesial consciousness brings a sense of belonging to *the mystery of the Church as Communion.* This is a basic and undeniable aspect of the life and mission of the Church. For one and all, the earnest prayer of Jesus at the Last Supper, *"That all may be one"* (Jn 17:21), ought to become daily a required and undeniable program of life and action.

A real sense of Church communion, the gift of the Spirit that urges our free and generous response, will bring forth as its precious fruit, in the "one and catholic" Church, the continuing value of the rich variety of vocations and conditions of life, charisms, ministries, works and responsibilities, as well as a more demonstrable and decisive collaboration of groups, associations and movements of the lay faithful in keeping with the accomplishment of the commonly shared salvific mission of the Church herself. This communion is already in itself the first great sign in the world of the presence of Christ the Savior. At the same time, it promotes and stimulates the proper apostolic and missionary action of the Church.

The whole Church, pastors and lay faithful alike, standing on the threshold of the Third Millennium, ought to feel more strongly the Church's responsibility to obey the command of Christ, "Go into all the world and preach the gospel to the whole creation" (Mk 16:15), and take up anew the missionary endeavor. A great venture, both challenging and wonderful, is entrusted to the Church—that of a *re-evangelization*, which is so much needed by the present world. The lay faithful ought to regard themselves as an active and responsible part of this venture, called as they are to proclaim and to live the Gospel in service to the person and to society while respecting the totality of the values and needs of both.

Since the Synod of Bishops was celebrated last October during the Marian Year, its work was entrusted in a very special way to the intercession of the Most Blessed Virgin Mary, Mother of the

Redeemer. I too entrust the spiritual fruitfulness of the Synod to her prayerful intercession. Therefore, along with the Synod Fathers, the lay faithful present at the Synod and all the other members of the People of God, I have recourse at the end of this post-Synodal document to the Virgin Mary. At this moment this appeal becomes a prayer:

O Most Blessed Virgin Mary,
Mother of Christ and Mother of the Church,
With joy and wonder we seek to make our own your *Magnificat*, joining you in your hymn of thankfulness and love.

With you we give thanks to God,
"whose mercy
is from generation to generation,"
for the exalted vocation
and the many forms of mission
entrusted to the lay faithful.
God has called each of them by name
to live his own communion of love
and holiness
and to be one
in the great family of God's children.
He has sent them forth
to shine with the light of Christ
and to communicate the fire of the Spirit
in every part of society
through their life
inspired by the Gospel.

O Virgin of the *Magnificat,*
fill their hearts
with a gratitude and enthusiasm
for this vocation and mission.

With humility and magnanimity
you were the "handmaid of the Lord";
give us your unreserved willingness
for service to God
and the salvation of the world.
Open our hearts
to the great anticipation
of the Kingdom of God
and of the proclamation of the Gospel
to the whole of creation.
Your mother's heart
is ever mindful of the many dangers
and evils which threaten
to overpower men and women
in our time.
At the same time your heart also takes notice
of the many initiatives
undertaken for good,
the great yearning for values,
and the progress achieved
in bringing forth
the abundant fruits of salvation.

O Virgin full of courage,
may your spiritual strength
and trust in God inspire us,
so that we might know
how to overcome all the obstacles
that we encounter
in accomplishing our mission.
Teach us to treat the affairs
of the world
with a real sense of Christian responsibility
and a joyful hope
of the coming of God's Kingdom, and
of a "new heavens and a new earth."

You who were gathered in prayer
with the Apostles in the Cenacle,
awaiting the coming
of the Spirit at Pentecost,
implore his renewed outpouring
on all the faithful, men and women alike,
so that they might more fully respond
to their vocation and mission,
as branches engrafted to the true vine,
called to bear much fruit
for the life of the world.

O Virgin Mother,
guide and sustain us
so that we might always live
as true sons and daughters
of the Church of your Son.
Enable us to do our part
in helping to establish on earth
the civilization of truth and love,
as God wills it,
for his glory.

Amen.

Given at Rome, in St. Peter's, on December 30, the Feast of the Holy Family of Jesus, Mary and Joseph, in the year 1988, the eleventh of my Pontificate.

Joannes Paulus PP. II

Notes

1. Second Vatican Ecumenical Council, Dogmatic Constitution on the Church *Lumen Gentium,* 48.

2. St. Gregory the Great, *Hom. in Evang.* 1, XIX, 2: *PL* 76, 1155.

3. Second Vatican Ecumenical Council, Decree on the Apostolate of Lay People *Apostolicam Actuositatem,* 33.

4. John Paul II, Homily at the Solemn Eucharistic Concelebration for the Close of the Seventh Ordinary General Assembly of the Synod of Bishops (October 30, 1987): *AAS* 80 (1988), 598.

5. Cf. *Propositio 1.*

6. Second Vatican Ecumenical Council, Pastoral Constitution on the Church in the Modern World *Gaudium et Spes,* 11.

7. The Fathers of the Extraordinary Synod of 1985, after affirming "the great importance and timeliness of the Pastoral Constitution, *Gaudium et Spes,"* continue: "Nevertheless, at the same time, they perceive that the signs of our times are in part different from those at the time of the Council with its problems and major trials. In fact, hunger, oppression, injustice and war, suffering, terrorism and forms of various kinds of violence are growing everywhere in the world today" *(Ecclesia sub Verbo Dei Mysteria Christi Celebrans pro salute Mundi. Relatio Finalis,* II, D, 1).

8. Second Vatican Ecumenical Council, Pastoral Constitution on the Church in the Modern World, *Gaudium et Spes,* 7.

9. St. Augustine, *Confessiones,* I, 1: *CCL* 27, 1.

10. Cf. *Instrumentum Laboris,* "The Vocation and Mission of the Lay Faithful in the Church and in the World Twenty Years after the Second Vatican Council," 5-10.

11. Second Vatican Ecumenical Council, Dogmatic Constitution on the Church *Lumen Gentium,* 1.

12. Second Vatican Ecumenical Council, Dogmatic Constitution on the Church *Lumen Gentium,* 6.

13. Cf. *Propositio 3.*

14. Second Vatican Ecumenical Council, Dogmatic Constitution on the Church *Lumen Gentium,* 31.

15. *Ibid.*

16. Pius XII, Discourse to the New Cardinals, February 20, 1946: *AAS* 38 (1946), 149.

17. Ecumenical Council of Florence, *Decr. pro Armeniis, DS* 1314.

18. Second Vatican Ecumenical Council, Dogmatic Constitution on the Church *Lumen Gentium,* 10.

19. St. Augustine, *Ennar. in Ps. XXVI,* II, 2: *CCL,* 38, 154ff.

20. Cf. Second Vatican Ecumenical Council, Dogmatic Constitution on the Church *Lumen Gentium,* 10.

21. John Paul II, Homily at the Beginning of his Pastoral Ministry as Supreme Shepherd of the Church (October 22, 1978): *AAS* 70 (1978), 946.

22. Cf. The renewed proposal of this teaching in the 1987 Synod's *Instrumentum Laboris,* "The Vocation and the Mission of the Lay Faithful in the Church and in the World Twenty Years after the Second Vatican Council," 25.

23. Second Vatican Ecumenical Council, Dogmatic Constitution on the Church *Lumen Gentium,* 34.

24. *Ibid.,* 35.

25. *Ibid.,* 12.

26. *Ibid.,* 35.

27. St. Augustine, *De Civitate Dei,* XX, 10: *CCL* 48, 720.

28. Second Vatican Ecumenical Council, Dogmatic Constitution on the Church *Lumen Gentium,* 32.

29. *Ibid.,* 31.

30. Paul VI, Talk to the Members of the Secular Institutes (February 2, 1972): *AAS* 64 (1972), 208.

31. Second Vatican Ecumenical Council, Decree on the Apostolate of Lay People *Apostolicam Actuositatem,* 5.

32. Second Vatican Ecumenical Council, Dogmatic Constitution on the Church *Lumen Gentium,* 31.

33. *Ibid.*

34. *Ibid.*

35. Cf. *ibid.,* 48.

36. Second Vatican Ecumenical Council, Pastoral Constitution on the Church in the Modern World, *Gaudium et Spes,* 32.

37. Second Vatican Ecumenical Council, Dogmatic Constitution on the Church *Lumen Gentium,* 31.

38. *Ibid.*

39. *Propositio 4.*

40. "Full members of the People of God and the Mystical Body, they participate, through Baptism, in the threefold priestly, prophetic and kingly mission of Christ; the lay faithful express and exercise the riches of their dignity through their *living in the world.* What can be an additional or exceptional task for those who belong to the ordained ministry is the *typical mission* of the lay faithful. *Their proper vocation* consists 'in seeking the Kingdom of God by engaging in temporal affairs and by ordering them according to the plan of God' *(Lumen Gentium,* 31)" (John Paul II, *Angelus* Talk, [March 15, 1987]: *Insegnamenti,* X, 1 [1987], 561).

41. See, in particular, the Dogmatic Constitution on the Church *Lumen Gentium,* 5, 39-42, which treats the subject of "the universal call to holiness in the Church."

42. The Second Extraordinary General Assembly of the Synod of Bishops (1985), *Ecclesia sub Verbo Dei Mysteria Christi Celebrans pro Salute Mundi. Relatio Finalis,* II, A, 4.

43. Second Vatican Ecumenical Council, Dogmatic Constitution on the Church *Lumen Gentium,* 40.

44. *Ibid.,* 42. These solemn and unequivocal affirmations of the Council repropose a fundamental truth of the Christian faith. Thus, for example, Pius XI in the Encyclical *Casti Connubii* addressed Christian spouses in the following words: "In whatever state they might be and whatever upright way of life they might have chosen, all must imitate the most perfect example of holiness, proposed by God to humanity, namely, our Lord Jesus Christ, and with the help of God to even reach the highest stage of Christian perfection, shown in the example of many saints": *AAS* 22 (1930), 548.

45. Second Vatican Ecumenical Council, Decree on the Apostolate of Lay People *Apostolicam Actuositatem,* 4.

46. *Propositio 5.*

47. *Propositio 8.*

48. St. Leo the Great, *Sermo XXI,* 3: *S. Ch.* 22a, 72.

49. S. Maximus, *Tract., III de Baptismo: PL* 57, 779.

50. St. Augustine, *In Ioann. Evang. Tract.*, 21, 8: *CCL* 36, 216.

51. Second Vatican Ecumenical Council, Dogmatic Constitution on the Church *Lumen Gentium*, 33.

52. Second Vatican Ecumenical Council, Dogmatic Constitution on the Church *Lumen Gentium*, 4.

53. The Second Extraordinary General Assembly of the Synod of Bishops (1985), *Ecclesia sub Verbo Dei Mysteria Christi Celebrans pro Salute Mundi. Relatio Finalis*, II, C. 1.

54. Paul VI, Wednesday General Audience Talk (June 8, 1966): *Insegnamenti*, IV (1966), 794.

55. Cf. Second Vatican Ecumenical Council, Dogmatic Constitution on the Church *Lumen Gentium*, 6.

56. Cf. *ibid.*, 7 *et passim.*

57. *Ibid.*, 9.

58. *Ibid.*, 1.

59. *Ibid.*, 9.

60. *Ibid.*, 7.

61. *Ibid.*

62. *Ibid.*, 4.

63. John Paul II, Homily at the Solemn Eucharistic Concelebration for the Close of the Seventh Ordinary General Assembly of the Synod of Bishops (October 30, 1987): *AAS* 80 (1988), 600.

64. Cf. Second Vatican Ecumenical Council, Dogmatic Constitution on the Church *Lumen Gentium*, 4.

65. Cf. Second Vatican Ecumenical Council, Decree on the Mission Activity of the Church *Ad Gentes*, 5.

66. Second Vatican Ecumenical Council, Decree on the Sacred Priesthood *Presbyterorum Ordinis*, 2; cf. Second Vatican Ecumenical Council, Dogmatic Constitution on the Church *Lumen Gentium*, 10.

67. Cf. Second Vatican Ecumenical Council, Dogmatic Constituion on the Church *Lumen Gentium*, 10.

68. Cf. John Paul II, Letter on Holy Thursday to all the Priests of the Church (April 9, 1979), 3-4: *Insegnamenti*, II, 1 (1979), 844-847.

69. Code of Canon Law, Can. 230 § 3.

70. Cf. Second Vatican Ecumenical Council, Decree on the Ministry and Life of Priests *Presbyterorum Ordinis*, 2 and 5.

71. Cf. Second Vatican Ecumenical Council, Decree on the Apostolate of Lay People *Apostolicam Actuositatem*, 24.

72. The Code of Canon Law lists a series of roles and tasks proper to the sacred ministers, that nevertheless for special and grave circumstances, and concretely in areas which lack priests or deacons, can temporarily be exercised by the lay faithful, with previous juridic faculty and mandated by competent ecclesiastical authority: cf. Can. 230 § 3; 517 § 2; 776; 861 § 2; 910 § 2; 943; § 1112, etc.

73. Cf. Second Vatican Ecumenical Council, Constitution on the Sacred Liturgy *Sacrosanctum Concilium*, 28; Code of Canon Law, Can. 230 § 2 that states: "lay persons can fulfill the function of lector during the liturgical actions by temporary deputation; likewise all lay persons can fulfill the functions of commentator or cantor or other functions, in accord with the norm of law."

74. The Code of Canon Law presents diverse roles and tasks that the lay faithful can fulfill in the organized structure of the Church: cf. Can. 228; 229 § 3; 317 § 3; 463 § 1; 5 and § 2; 483; 494; 537; 759; 776; 784; 785; 1282; 1421.

75. Cf. *Propositio 18.*

76. Paul VI, Apostolic Exhortation *Evangelii Nuntiandi,* 70: *AAS* 68 (1976), 60.

77. Cf. Code of Canon Law, Can 230 § 1.

78. *Propositio 18.*

79. Second Vatican Ecumenical Council, Decree on the Apostolate of Lay People *Apostolicam Actuositatem*, 3.

80. "From the reception of these charisms or gifts, even the most ordinary ones, there arises for each believer the right and duty to use them in the Church and in the world for the good of people and the building up of the Church. In doing so believers need to enjoy the freedom of the Holy Spirit who 'breathes where he wills' (Jn 3:8). At the same time they much act in communion with their brothers and sisters in Christ, especially with their Pastor" *(ibid.).*

81. *Propositio 9.*

82. Second Vatican Ecumenical Council, Dogmatic Constitution on the Church *Lumen Gentium,* 12.

83. Cf. *ibid.,* 30.

84. Second Vatican Ecumenical Council, Decree on the Pastoral Office of Bishops in the Church *Christus Dominus,* 11.

85. Second Vatican Ecumenical Council, Dogmatic Constitution on the Church *Lumen Gentium*, 23.

86. Second Vatican Ecumenical Council, Decree on the Apostolate of Lay People *Apostolicam Actuositatem*, 10.

87. Cf. *Propositio 10*.

88. Cf. Code of Canon Law, Can. 443 § 4; 463 § 1 and § 2.

89. Cf. *Propositio 10*.

90. The Council documents read: "It is impossible for the bishop always and everywhere to preside over the whole flock in his Church, he must of necessity establish groupings of the faithful. Among these, parishes set up locally under a pastor who takes the place of the bishop are the most important: for in a certain way they represent the visible Church as it is established throughout the world" (Second Vatican Ecumenical Council, Constitution on the Sacred Liturgy *Sacrosanctum Concilium*, 42).

91. Second Vatican Ecumenical Council, Dogmatic Constitution on the Church, *Lumen Gentium*, 28.

92. John Paul II, Apostolic Exhortation *Catechesi Tradendae*, 67: *AAS* 71 (1979), 1333.

93. Code of Canon Law, Can. 515 § 1.

94. Cf. *Propositio 10*.

95. Cf. Second Vatican Ecumenical Council, Constitution on the Sacred Liturgy *Sacrosanctum Concilium*, 42).

96. Cf. Code of Canon Law, Can 555 § 1, 1.

97. Cf. Code of Canon Law, Can. 383 § 1.

98. Paul VI, Discourse to the Roman Clergy (June 24, 1963): *AAS* 55 (1963), 674.

99. *Propositio 11*.

100. Second Vatican Ecumenical Council, Decree on the Apostolate of Lay People *Apostolicam Actuositatem*, 10.

101. *Ibid.*

102. Cf. *Propositio 10*.

103. St. Gregory the Great, *Hom. in Ez.*, II, I, 5: *CCL* 142, 211.

104. Second Vatican Ecumenical Council, Decree on the Apostolate of Lay People *Apostolicam Actuositatem*, 16.

105. John Paul II, *Angelus* Talk (August 23, 1987): *Insegnamenti*, X, 3 (1987), 240.

106. Second Vatican Ecumenical Council, Decree on the Apostolate of Lay People *Apostolicam Actuositatem*, 18.

107. *Ibid.*, 19; cf. also *ibid.*, 15; Second Vatican Ecumenical Council, Dogmatic Constitution on the Church *Lumen Gentium*, 37.

108. Code of Canon Law, Can. 215.

109. Second Vatican Ecumenical Council, Dogmatic Constitution on the Church *Lumen Gentium*, 39.

110. Cf. *ibid.*, 40.

111. Second Vatican Ecumenical Council, Decree on the Apostolate of Lay People *Apostolicam Actuositatem*, 19.

112. Cf. Second Vatican Ecumenical Council, Dogmatic Constitution on the Church *Lumen Gentium*, 23.

113. *Ibid.*

114. Second Vatican Ecumenical Council, Decree on the Apostolate of Lay People *Apostolicam Actuositatem*, 23.

115. *Ibid.*, 20.

116. *Ibid.*, 24.

117. *Propositio 13.*

118. Cf. *Propositio 15.*

119. John Paul II, Discourse at a Meeting of the Church in Loreto, Italy, (April 10, 1985): *AAS* 77 (1985), 964.

120. Second Vatican Ecumenical Council, Dogmatic Constitution on the Church *Lumen Gentium*, 1.

121. *Ibid.*, 30.

122. Second Vatican Ecumenical Council, Decree on the Apostolate of Lay People *Apostolicam Actuositatem*, 10.

123. Paul VI, *Evangelii Nuntiandi*, 14: *AAS* 68 (1976), 13.

124. John Paul II, Homily of His Holiness at the Beginning of His Ministry as Supreme Shepherd of the Church (October 22, 1978): *AAS* 70 (1978), 947.

125. *Propositio 10.*

126. Second Vatican Ecumenical Council, Decree on the Mission Activity of the Church *Ad Gentes*, 20; cf. also *ibid.*, 37.

127. *Propositio 29.*

128. Cf. Second Vatican Ecumenical Council, Decree on the Mission Activity of the Church *Ad Gentes*, 21.

129. *Propositio 30 bis.*

130. Second Vatican Ecumenical Council, Dogmatic Constitution on the Church *Lumen Gentium*, 5.

131. Cf. Second Vatican Ecumenical Council, Pastoral Constitution on the Church in the Modern World *Gaudium et Spes*, 22.

132. *Ibid.*, 22.

133. John Paul II, Encyclical Letter *Redemptor Hominis*, 14: *AAS* 71 (1979), 284-285.

134. Second Vatican Ecumenical Council, Pastoral Constitution on the Church in the Modern World *Gaudium et Spes*, 40.

135. Cf. *ibid.*, 12.

136. "If we celebrate so solemnly the birth of Jesus, we do it so as to bear witness to the fact that each person is someone, unique and irrepeatable. If humanity's statistics and arrangement, its political, economic and social systems as well as its simple possibilities, do not come about to assure man that he can be born, exist and work as a unique and irrepeatable individual, then bid 'farewell' to all assurances. For Christ and because of him, the individual is always unique and irrepeatable; someone eternally conceived and eternally chosen; someone called and given a special name" (John Paul II, First Christmas Radio Message to the World: *AAS* 71 [1979], 66).

137. Second Vatican Ecumenical Council, Pastoral Constitution on the Church in the Modern World *Gaudium et Spes*, 27.

138. John Paul II, Apostolic Exhortation *Familiaris Consortio*, 30: *AAS* 74 (1982), 116.

139. Cf. Congregation for the Doctrine of the Faith, Instruction on Respect for Human Life in its Origin and on the Dignity of Procreation: Replies to Certain Questions of the Day *Donum Vitae* (March 11, 1987): *AAS* 80 (1988), 70-102.

140. *Propositio 36.*

141. John Paul II, Message for the Twenty-first World Day of Peace, "Religious Freedom: Condition for Peace" (December 8, 1987): *AAS* 80 (1988), 278, 280.

142. St. Augustine, *De Catech. Rud.*, XXIV, 44: *CCL* 46, 168.

143. *Propositio 32.*

144. Second Vatican Ecumenical Council, Pastoral Constitution on the Church in the Modern World *Gaudium et Spes*, 24.

145. *Ibid.*, 12.

146. Cf. John Paul II, Apostolic Exhortation, *Familiaris Consortio,* 42-48: *AAS* 74 (1982), 134-140.

147. *Ibid.*, 85: *AAS* 74 (1982), 188.

148. Second Vatican Ecumenical Council, Decree on the Apostolate of Lay People *Apostolicam Actuositatem,* 8.

149. For the relationship between justice and mercy, see John Paul II, Encyclical Letter *Dives in Misericordia,* 12: *AAS* 72 (1980), 1215-1217.

150. Second Vatican Ecumenical Council, Pastoral Constitution on the Church in the Modern World *Gaudium et Spes*, 75.

151. *Ibid.*, 74.

152. *Ibid.*, 76.

153. Cf. *Propositio 28.*

154. John Paul II, Encyclical Letter *Sollicitudo Rei Socialis,* 38: *AAS* 80 (1988), 565-566.

155. Cf. John XXIII, Encyclical Letter *Pacem in Terris: AAS* 55 (1963), 265-266.

156. John Paul II, Encyclical Letter *Sollicitudo Rei Socialis,* 39: *AAS* 80 (1988), 568.

157. Cf. *Propositio 26.*

158. Second Vatican Ecumenical Council, Pastoral Constitution on the Church in the Modern World *Gaudium et Spes*, 63.

159. Cf. *Propositio 24.*

160. Second Vatican Ecumenical Council, Pastoral Constitution on the Church in the Modern World *Gaudium et Spes*, 67.

161. John Paul II, Encyclical Letter *Sollicitudo Rei Socialis,* 34: *AAS* 80 (1988), 560.

162. Second Vatican Ecumenical Council, Pastoral Constitution on the Church in the Modern World *Gaudium et Spes*, 53.

163. Cf. *Propositio 35.*

164. Second Vatican Ecumenical Council, Pastoral Constitution on the Church in the Modern World *Gaudium et Spes*, 58.

165. Paul VI, Apostolic Exhortation, *Evangelii Nuntiandi,* 18-20: *AAS* 68 (1976), 18-19.

166. Cf. *Propositio 37.*

167. St. Gregory the Great, *Hom. in Evang.* I, XIX, 2: *PL* 76, 1155.

168. Second Vatican Ecumenical Council, Declaration on Christian Education *Gravissimum Educationis,* 2.

169. John Paul II, Apostolic Letter for the "International Year of Youth," 15: *AAS* 77 (1985), 620-621.

170. *Propositio 52.*

171. *Propositio 51.*

172. Second Vatican Ecumenical Council, Message to Youth (December 8, 1965): *AAS* 58 (1966), 18.

173. Second Vatican Ecumenical Council, Pastoral Constitution on the Church in the Modern World *Gaudium et Spes,* 48.

174. John Gerson, *De Parvulis ad Christum Trahendis. Œuvres Complètes,* Desclée, Paris 1973, IX, 669.

175. John Paul II, Discourse to a Gathering of Older People from the Dioceses of Italy (March 23, 1984): *Insegnamenti,* VII, 1 (1984), 744.

176. Cf. John XXIII, Encyclical Letter *Pacem in Terris: AAS* 55 (1963), 267-268.

177. John Paul II, Apostolic Exhortation *Familiaris Consortio,* 24: *AAS* 74 (1982), 109-110.

178. *Propositio 46.*

179. *Propositio 47.*

180. Second Vatican Ecumenical Council, Decree on the Apostolate of Lay People *Apostolicam Actuositatem,* 9.

181. Paul VI, Discourse to the Committee for the International Year of the Woman (April 18, 1975): *AAS* 67 (1975), 266.

182. *Propositio 46.*

183. *Propositio 47.*

184. *Ibid.*

185. Second Vatican Ecumenical Council, Pastoral Constitution on the Church in the Modern World *Gaudium et Spes,* 10.

186. The Encyclical Letter *Redemptoris Mater,* after having recalled that the "Marian dimension of the Christian life takes on a particular importance in relation to women and their status," states, "In fact, femininity has a *unique relationship* with the Mother of the Redeemer, a subject which can be studied in greater depth elsewhere. Here I simply wish to note that the example of Mary of Nazareth sheds light on *woman-*

hood as such by the very fact that God, in the sublime event of the Incarnation of his Son, entrusted himself to the ministry, the free and active ministry of a woman. It can thus be said that women, by looking to Mary, find in her the secret of living their femininity with dignity and of achieving their own true advancement. In the light of Mary, the Church sees in women the reflection of a beauty which mirrors the loftiest sentiments of which the human heart is capable: the totality of the gift of self in love; the strength that is capable of bearing the greatest sorrows; limitless fidelity and tireless devotion to work; the ability to combine penetrating intuition with words, support and encouragement" (John Paul II, Encyclical Letter *Redemptoris Mater,* 46: *AAS* 79 [1987], 424-425).

187. John Paul II, Apostolic Letter *Mulieris Dignitatem,* 16.

188. Cf. Congregation for the Doctrine of the Faith, Declaration on the Question of Admission of Women to the Ministerial Priesthood *Inter Insigniores* (October 15, 1976): *AAS* 69 (1977), 98-116.

189. Cf. John Paul II, Apostolic Letter *Mulieris Dignitatem,* 26.

190. *Ibid.,* 27; "The Church is a differentiated body in which each individual has a role; the tasks are distinct and must not be confused; they do not favor the superiority of one over the other, nor do they provide an excuse for jealousy; the only better gift, which can and must be desired is love (cf. 1 Cor 12–13). The greatest in the Kingdom of Heaven are not the ministers but the saints" (Congregation for the Doctrine of the Faith, Declaration on the Question of Admission of Women to the Ministerial Priesthood *Inter Insigniores* [October 15, 1976], 6: *AAS* 69 [1977], 115).

191. Paul VI, Discourse to the Committee for the International Women's Year (April 18, 1975): *AAS* 67 (1975), 266.

192. *Propositio 47.*

193. *Ibid.*

194. Second Vatican Ecumenical Council, Dogmatic Constitution on the Church *Lumen Gentium,* 36.

195. John Paul II, Apostolic Exhortation *Familiaris Consortio,* 50: *AAS* 74 (1982), 141-142.

196. *Propositio 46.*

197. *Propositio 47.*

198. The Seventh Ordinary General Assembly of the Synod of Bishops (1987), *Per Concilii semitas ad Populum Dei Nuntius,* 12.

199. *Propositio 53.*

200. John Paul II, Apostolic Letter *Salvifici Doloris,* 3: *AAS* 76 (1984), 203.

201. St. Ignatius of Antioch, *Ad Ephesios,* VII, 2: *S. Ch.* 10, 64.

202. John Paul II, Apostolic Letter *Salvifici Doloris,* 31: *AAS* 76 (1984), 249-250.

203. St. Ambrose, *De Virginitate,* VI, 34: *PL* 16, 288; cf. St. Augustine, *Sermo CCCIV,* III, 2: *PL* 38, 1396.

204. Cf. Pius XII, Apostolic Constitution, *Provida Mater* (February 2, 1947): *AAS* 39 (1947), 114-124; Code of Canon Law, Can. 573.

205. *Propositio 6.*

206. Cf. Paul VI, Apostolic Letter *Sabaudiae Gemma* (January 29, 1967): *AAS* 59 (1967), 113-123.

207. St. Francis de Sales, *Introduction à la vie dévote,* I, III: *(Œuvres complètes,* Monastère de la Visitation, Annecy 1983, III, 19-21.

208. Second Vatican Ecumenical Council, Decree on the Apostolate of Lay People *Apostolicam Actuositatem,* 4.

209. *Propositio 40.*

210. *Dabit virtutem, qui contulit dignitatem!* (St. Leo the Great, *Serm.* II, 1: *S. Ch.* 200, 248).

211. Second Vatican Ecumenical Council, Decree on the Apostolate of Lay People *Apostolicam Actuositatem,* 4.

212. Second Vatican Ecumenical Council, Pastoral Constitution on the Church in the Modern World *Gaudium et Spes,* 43; cf. also, Second Vatican Ecumenical Council, Decree on the Mission Activity of the Church *Ad Gentes,* 21; Paul VI, Apostolic Exhortation *Evangelii Nuntiandi,* 20: *AAS* 68 (1976), 19.

213. John Paul II, Discourse to the Participants in the National Congress of Church Movements of Cultural Responsibility (M.E.I.C.) (January 16, 1982), 2: *Insegnamenti,* V, 1 (1982), 131; Also Letter to Cardinal Agostino Casaroli, Secretary of State, establishing the Pontifical Council for Culture (May 20, 1982): *AAS* 74 (1982), 685; Discourse to the Community of the University of Louvain (May 20, 1985), 2: *Insegnamenti,* VIII, 1 (1985), 1591.

214. Second Vatican Ecumenical Council, Decree on the Apostolate of Lay People *Apostolicam Actuositatem,* 4.

215. *Propositio 22;* cf. also John Paul II, Encyclical *Sollicitudo Rei Socialis,* 41: *AAS* 80 (1988), 570-572.

216. Second Vatican Ecumenical Council, Decree on the Apostolate of Lay People *Apostolicam Actuositatem,* 4.

217. St. Methodius of Olympo, *Symposion III,* 8: *S. Ch.* 95, 110.

218. Cf. *Propositio 11.*

219. *Propositio 40.*

220. Cf. *Propositio 44.*

221. Cf. *Propositio 45.*

222. *Propositio 44.*

223. *Propositio 41.*

224. *Propositio 42.*

BOOKS & MEDIA

The Daughters of St. Paul operate book and media centers at the following addresses. Visit, call or write the one nearest you today, or find us on the World Wide Web, www.pauline.org

California
3908 Sepulveda Blvd., Culver City, CA 90230; 310-397-8676
5945 Balboa Ave., San Diego, CA 92111; 858-565-9181
46 Geary Street, San Francisco, CA 94108; 415-781-5180

Florida
145 S.W. 107th Ave., Miami, FL 33174; 305-559-6715

Hawaii
1143 Bishop Street, Honolulu, HI 96813; 808-521-2731

Neighbor Islands call: 800-259-8463

Illinois
172 North Michigan Ave., Chicago, IL 60601; 312-346-4228

Louisiana
4403 Veterans Memorial Blvd., Metairie, LA 70006; 504-887-7631

Massachusetts
Rte. 1, 885 Providence Hwy., Dedham, MA 02026; 781-326-5385

Missouri
9804 Watson Rd., St. Louis, MO 63126; 314-965-3512

New Jersey
561 U.S. Route 1, Wick Plaza, Edison, NJ 08817; 732-572-1200

New York
150 East 52nd Street, New York, NY 10022; 212-754-1110
78 Fort Place, Staten Island, NY 10301; 718-447-5071

Ohio
2105 Ontario Street, Cleveland, OH 44115; 216-621-9427

Pennsylvania
9171-A Roosevelt Blvd., Philadelphia, PA 19114; 215-676-9494

South Carolina
243 King Street, Charleston, SC 29401; 843-577-0175

Tennessee
4811 Poplar Ave., Memphis, TN 38117; 901-761-2987

Texas
114 Main Plaza, San Antonio, TX 78205; 210-224-8101

Virginia
1025 King Street, Alexandria, VA 22314; 703-549-3806

Canada
3022 Dufferin Street, Toronto, Ontario, Canada M6B 3T5; 416-781-9131
1155 Yonge Street, Toronto, Ontario, Canada M4T 1W2; 416-934-3440

¡También somos su fuente para libros, videos y música en español!